MW01503431

WHO'S WALKING *with* YOU?

Erma Hershberger

A study guide highlighting God's blessings and our
need for them in our walk with Christ

WHO'S WALKING WITH YOU?

ISBN 0-9741636-0-0

Erma Hershberger
29991 CR 236
Fresno, OH 43824

© 2003 Dan and Erma Hershberger

All rights reserved. No portion of this book may be reproduced
by any means, electronic or mechanical, including photocopying,
recording, or by any information storage retrieval system, without permission
of the copyright's owner, except for the inclusion of brief quotations for a review.

Scripture quotations taken from the New American Standard Bible®,
Copyright©1960, 1962, 1963, 1968, 1971, 1972, 1973,
1975, 1977, 1995 by The Lockman Foundation.
Used by permission. www.Lockman.org

A special thanks and appreciation:

To Dan
who encouraged me,
and helped me in many countless ways.
Much of what is written in the pages
to follow is as much his understanding as mine.

To Darlene
who faithfully proofread every page

To Dave Ernst
who drew the picture for the cover

To Susie
who helped me in understanding the computer

To my children
who listened to and encouraged me

To the countless others who urged me on.
Thank-You

Contents – Verses

Blessings –vers. Curses

Eternal Life ----------- Death
Truth ------------------- Lies
Hope -------------------- Despair
Faith ------------------- Presumption

Love -------------------- Hate
Forgiveness ----------- Bitterness
Peace ------------------- Turmoil
Joy ---------------------- Stumbling
Strength ---------------- Condemnation
Confidence ----------- Unprepared

Vision ----------------- Blind
Purpose ---------------- Useless
Beloved --------------- Rejection
Blessings ------------- Curses

Repentance ---------- Frustration
Humility ------------- Pride
Prayer ---------------- Confusion

Patience ------------- Anger
Authority ---------- Irresponsible
Soldier -------------- Carnal

Righteousness --- Sin
Favor -------------- Dishonesty
Grace -------------- Stress
Discernment ------ Ignorance

Holy Spirit -------- Chance
Anointing --------- Self
Word of God ------ Emptiness
Wisdom ----------- Jealousy
Knowledge ------- Carelessness

Virtue ----------- Anxious

Health ---------------- Sickness

Goodness ------------ Evil
Gentleness ----------- Harsh
Meekness------------- Boastful
Endurance ------------ Overwhelmed

Tongues --------------- Oppression
Courage --------------- Discouragement
Friend of God -------- Fearful
Compassion ----------- Cruel

Self-Control ----------- Chaos
Perseverance ---------- Procrastination
Godliness -------------- Worldliness
Unconditional love --- Lost
Sabbath Rest ---------- Struggling

Pure -------------------- Defiled
Devout ----------------- Ineffective
Fear of God ----------- Foolishness

Honor ------------------ Dishonor
Dignity ---------------- Slave
Understanding -------- Darkness
Skilled Workman ----- Lazy

Thankful --------------- Futile
Influence -------------- Unwise
Steward ---------------- Unfaithful
Good Reputation ------ Unreliable

Fruit ---------------------- Filthy Rags

Chronological Order

Who's Walking With You?

Behold, it is the traveling couch of Solomon;
Threescore mighty men are about it,
Of the mighty men of Israel.
They all handle the sword, and are expert in war:
Every man hath his sword upon his thigh,
Because of fear in the night.
Song of Solomon 3:7,8

This book is written for these who have given themselves to be disciples of Jesus Christ. A disciple is one who subscribes to the teachings of a master and assists in spreading them. Jesus said, "If you abide in My word, then you are truly disciples of Mine."   In Luke 14:25-33, we find the cost of being a disciple of Jesus'. But let me assure you, God never commands us to do anything, but that he makes a way to do it, and provides the provision, I Corinthians 10:13.

A number of years ago, while studying for a Bible Study, I came across a verse that caught my attention. Song of Solomon 3:7, "Behold, it is the traveling couch of Solomon; sixty mighty men around it, of the mighty men of Israel." Now Solomon was king of Israel, and this is how the bride saw him coming. He was not walking alone. Neither should we walk alone, I thought. I took a quarter and drew this picture that was forming in my mind. If he was on a traveling couch, four men were carrying him. I imagine it as a chair with poles along the sides to be carried. Then as I continued, I understood that he had fourteen men walking before him, fourteen men behind, and fourteen men on both sides. He was well protected. Nothing could get to him without encountering these men first, and they were mighty men of Israel.

Now I had this paper with sixty empty circles on it. What were the names of these men? So this was homework for the following week. Each lady received a paper of circles, and she was to decide who she would want carrying her, who should be walking before her, behind and beside her. And I told them, we were thinking of blessings that we would want in our lives. This I did with four different Bible Studies and I recorded all the different blessings that came in with each group. I ended up with 150 different names of blessings. From these all together I then tried to take the basic ones to make a chart. Blessings we all need walking with us, because we do have somebody walking along side of us either good or evil.

I used this chart as a prayer guide, asking the Lord to place these blessings in my life. Then one day I read the next verse. I'm sure I had read it before, but this time it caught my attention. Song of Solomon 3:8, "All of them were wielders of the sword, expert in war, each man has his sword at his side, guarding against the terrors of the night." With men like that walking before, behind and beside me, I would feel pretty safe. There is a way to place these blessings into our lives and have them become flesh, a part of us. Each one of these men needs a sword by his side. The sword of the Spirit, which is the Word of God, Ephesians 6:17.

When you memorize a verse of scripture, it does a work in your life. In order to memorize a verse, so that it will stick with you, this is what you need to do. You read it, make sure you understand every word. If there are words you are not sure of, look them up in the dictionary. Think, what is this verse saying, what is the concept. Read the chapter of the verse, get the setting. Every scripture has a promise for you, what is the promise? To attain that promise, there is always a condition to meet. Find the condition and act upon it. It's when we hear the Word and act upon it, that we can be compared to a wise man, who built his house on a rock, Matthew 7:24.

The first and greatest blessing in our lives is humility. It is the root of all the rest. When we have humility in our lives, we then walk with a right attitude before God, which allows God to be God. It's alright if I'm not always right. Being humble has to do with having a teachable spirit. Always being ready to learn and better myself. Leaning on God.

God walked with Adam, Enoch walked with God. Abraham walked before God, he was a friend of God. Who is walking with you? (walk means - to move over a surface by taking steps with the feet at a pace slower than a run). God through His divine power has granted to us everything pertaining to life and godliness, everything we need to live and to live in a godly way. He has blessed us with every spiritual blessing in heavenly places. How do we walk (move, take steps) in these blessings given to us. Who is walking with you? Do you choose your friends? Or do you invite anything that happens to come your way? Is fear walking with you? God would want you to have power, love, and a sound mind to walk with you? You have the right to choose. As a child of the King, choose royalty.

In Song of Solomon, the bride was looking for her bridegroom. She found him, coming out of the wilderness, with columns of smoke, perfumed with myrrh and frankincense. Behold, the traveling couch of Solomon. He was a king. Yes, a king. So are you, we are priests and kings unto God, Rev.1:6.

Sixty mighty men were around this traveling couch of Solomon's. (Mighty means - having or showing great power, skill, strength or force). He had gathered around himself sixty mighty men of Israel. He did not walk alone. These were, all of them, able to handle the sword. They knew how to use a sword and were expert in war. Every man had his sword on his thigh, because of fear in the night. These sixty, Solomon gathered around himself to go through life with him. He did not try to walk this journey alone. And they all carried swords. The Word of God is a sword that is living, active, and sharper than a two-edged sword. A sword that cuts and judges the thoughts and the intentions of the heart, Hebrews 4:12. What mighty men do you chose to walk with you? And what swords do they carry?

Each one of these men (blessings) is backed with a verse of Scripture. That's the sword he is carrying. Eph.1:3, "Blessed be the God and Father of our Lord Jesus Christ, who has blessed us with every spiritual blessing in the heavenly places in Christ." God has blessed us with every blessing there is. All we need for every circumstance that could ever arise. Blessings more mighty than the mighty men of Solomon. So I believe the story of Solomon was for us. Do you know who is walking with you? God has a blessing to fill every spot to surround you, just as Solomon's sixty mighty men surrounded him.

It was a traveling couch, the bride saw as she looked toward the wilderness. This took four men to carry it. There were fourteen men going before him, fourteen men on either side, fourteen men behind him. As we fill each place with a blessing, we need to know a Word of God to make it become a part of us. Knowing a verse, reading it, meditating on it, memorizing it until we understand it in our heart. As we do that, it becomes a Sword to protect us from evil.

When Jesus was leaving this earth, He told His disciples He would leave and the Comforter, (Holy Spirit) would come and He would teach you all things. Whatever situation might arise in our lives, we can always hear from God. Ask and you shall receive, seek and you shall find, knock and the door will be opened, Matthew 7:8. When we still our hearts, and wait on Him in prayer, the Holy Spirit will quicken a word to us, a word appropriate for our victory that will give us a vision on how to precede. We then look for the condition concerning this promise, be obedient in doing whatever that is, and the promise will be yours. This is faith in action.

God has prepared for you a couch. He has four mighty men (blessings) to carry you through life. Put yourself now on this traveling couch. Let God's promises carry you, surround you, as you journey through this time on earth. We are only here for a time. God has a plan for us, Jeremiah 29:11. "For I know the thoughts that I think toward you, saith Jehovah, thoughts of peace, and not in evil, to give you hope in your latter end." We are going to "a city, whose architect and builder is God" Heb.11:10.

As you work your way through this book, surrounding yourself with the blessings of God. You will want to gather around each of yourself sixty men (blessings) of God, by taking a verse of Scripture, seeing the promise in it, understanding the condition connected to it, then fulfilling the condition. Let the Word become flesh, a part of you! This is agreeing with God.

If we do not have God's Blessings around us, we have evil hindrances surrounding us. I have tried to illustrate this in diagram. I will not amplify on that, since we always want to dwell on the good and not the evil. But know this, there is someone who is walking with you. If you have not placed blessings in your life, evil is there.

In Romans 3:23, the Word says, we have all sinned and fall short of the glory of God. Sin is many times just as much what we don't do as what we do. Sin came into the world when Eve made a decision on her own, without consulting God. Then Adam did the same. God wants us to be dependent on Him.

Take your time to work through this book, taking a topic at a time. Take time to memorize the verse. Read the entire chapter from where it is taken. Look up any words you might not understand in the dictionary. Write the verse on a card. Carry it with you, repeat it many times a day. Be sure to memorize the reference. In doing this, it will become a part of you. The Word will become flesh (John 1:14) (Christ in you). Matthews 7:24, "Everyone therefore that heareth these words of Mine, and doeth them, shall be likened unto a wise man, who built his house upon the rock" This is the key to become a wise person, to hear the Scripture and do it.

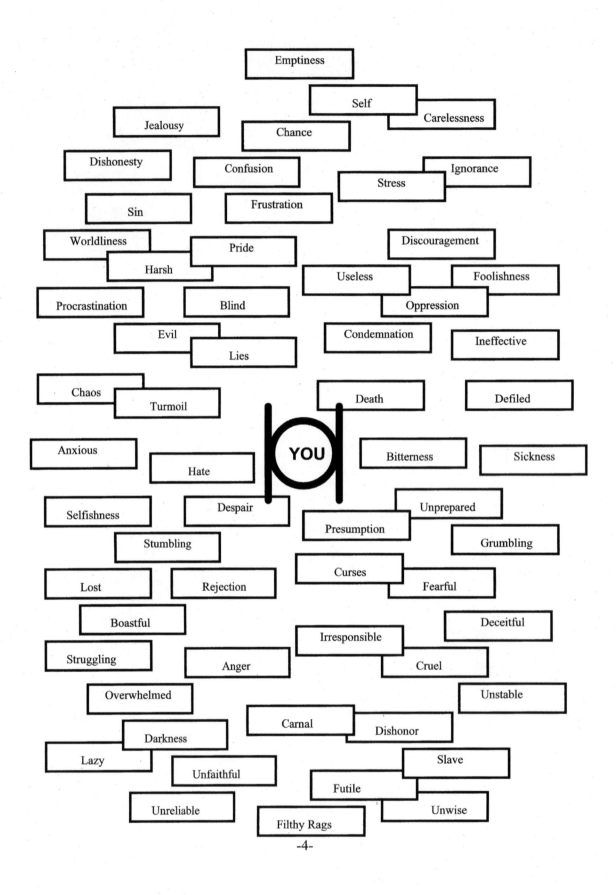

A Life in Need

**for all have sinned and fall short
of the glory of God
Romans 3:23**

As you start your journey through this book, this first page is here to show you how your life looks without the blessings of God. As you place a blessing into your life, the opposite is taken away, until we come to the end where we only see blessings. The blessings are symbolized in circles, the evil which just naturally walks around you if you don't make an effort to replace them, which are symbolized by rectangles.

Take your time to go through this journey. Use a notebook of your own to write down what God would share with you about each one. Many of these blessings have had books written about them. And those that don't, could have. Be sure to look up every reference that's mentioned, it is needed to get the thought, that I am writing to you.

Be prayerful as to how you can apply this to your every day life. I have used much more facts than application. I'm trusting the Holy Spirit to teach you, to guide you and to equip you, so that you will understand how to apply it to your life.

Be sure to spend much time reading the chapter the verse is taken from. Read it until you see the need of having the blessing in your life. If you feel you already have this particular blessing in you life, thank God for it.

When you see the need in your life for the blessing you're reading about. Ask God to give it to you. Repent, and ask forgiveness for the opposite (sin) you are living with. Be humble (teachable), understanding brings light into a situation. Watch yourself respond to things that would indicate that the blessing is there.

Be sure to write the verse on a card. Buy a key ring, and then put all your cards on this ring after you have learned them. Go over them from time to time. This book is written with the intend of getting you into the Word of God. It can be used as a Bible Study guide, either on a individual basis or as a group.

The Promise: The Condition: Psalm One Blessed is the man that walketh not in the counsel of the wicked, Nor standeth in the way of sinners, Nor sitteth in the seat of scoffers: But his delight is in the law of Jehovah; And on his law doth he meditate day and night. And he shall be like a tree planted by the streams of water, That bringeth forth its fruit in its season, Whose leaf also doth not wither; And whatsoever he doeth shall prosper. The wicked are not so, But are like the chaff which the wind driveth away. Therefore the wicked shall not stand in the judgment, Nor sinners in the congregation of the righteous. For Jehovah knoweth the way of the righteous; But the way of the wicked shall perish.

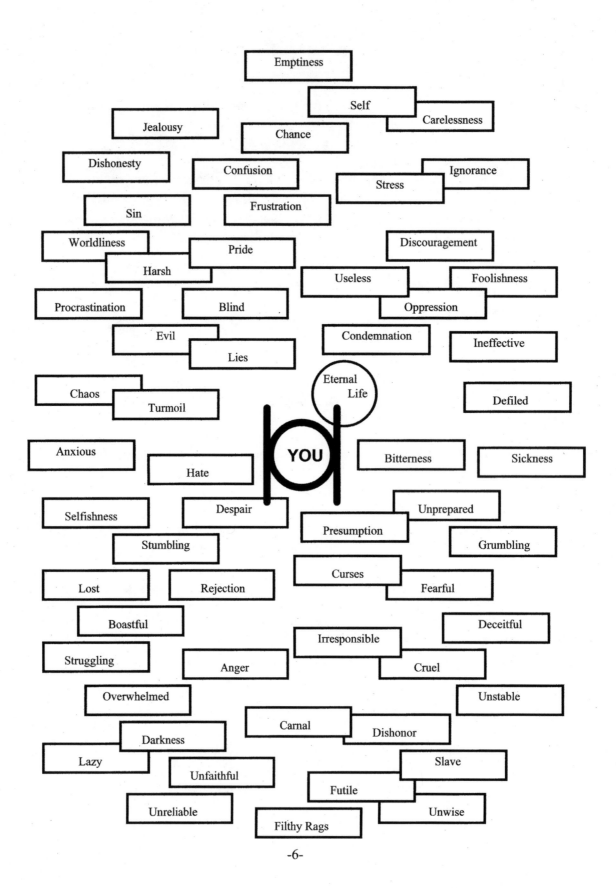

-6-

Eternal Life

And this is Life Eternal,
that they should know Thee
the only true God,
and Him whom thou didst send,
even Jesus Christ.
John 17:3

John 17, a prayer, that Jesus prayed for His disciples and all those who believe through their word. We read in John 13 of the last supper. Jesus spoke many basic truths in the chapters that follow. In (ch.14:31), "arise let us go from here," He said. They went to the Garden, but Jesus continued with His last words. Here in chapter seventeen He started to pray.

He prayed that we might have eternal life, and explained that to know the Father, the only true God is having eternal life. When Jesus started to preach three years earlier, He said, "Repent, for the kingdom of heaven is at hand. And He started to teach them the ways of the kingdom.

But his mission for coming to earth is found in I Cor.15:3 and 4. He came to die for our sins, He was buried, He was raised on the third day. He has paid the price of all sin, yours and mine alike. As we accept Him as overcoming on our behalf, we can come into peace with God our Father in heaven.

How do you accept Christ?
1) Admit your need (I am a sinner).
2) Be willing to turn from your sins (repent)
3) Believe that Jesus Christ died for you on the cross, was buried and rose from the grave.
4) Through prayer, invite Jesus Christ to come in and control your life through the Holy Spirit. (Receive Him as Lord and Savior).

Pray: Dear Lord Jesus,
I know that I am a sinner and need Your forgiveness. I believe that You died for my sins. I want to turn from my sins. I now invite You to come into my heart and life. I want to trust and follow You as Lord and Savior.   In Jesus' name, Amen

The Promise: eternal life; peace with the Father

The Condition: walking the Romans Road; (3:10) no one righteous; (3:23) all have sinned; (5:12) through one man's death - all died; (6:23) wages of sin is death; gift of God is eternal life; (5:8) God's love, Christ died; (10:9,10,13) confess with mouth, believe in heart, you shall be saved.

Take time to memorize the verse. Write it on a card, carry it with you, repeat it many times a day. Also memorize the reference. Read the entire chapter of John 17, every day this week.
Let the word become flesh - a part of you!

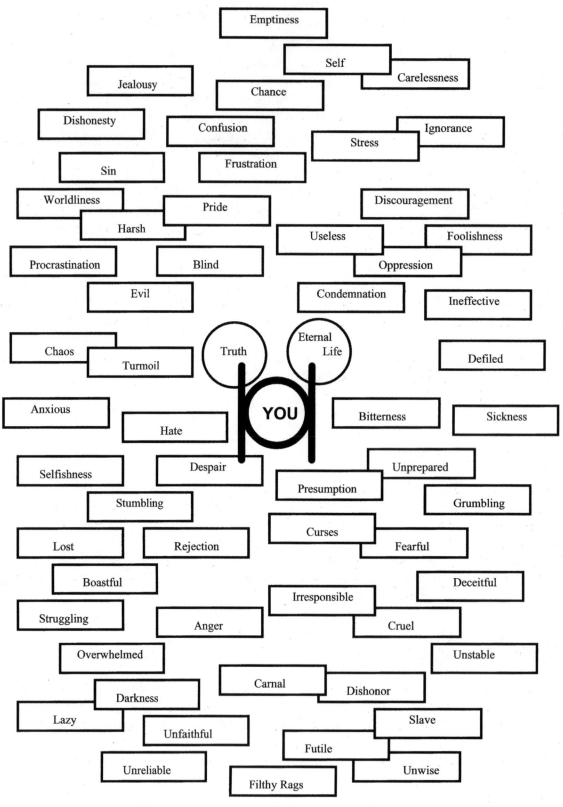

Truth

**If you abide in My Word,
then you are truly disciples of Mine:
and ye shall know the Truth,
and the Truth shall make you free.
John 8:31,32**

A disciple is one who subscribes to the teachings of a master and assists in spreading them. If we want to be a disciple we must know our master and what He teaches. The Bible is the Word of God. It is important that you read the Bible. Also that you learn the order in which the books come in. There are 66 books in the Bible; 39 make up the Old Testament, and 27 the New Testament.

There is much truth in this passage of Scripture that we need to take heed of. First He shows us that He will not condemn the sinner, but He tells them, "go and sin no more." In verse 12, "I am the light of the world; he who follows Me shall not walk in the darkness, but shall have the light of life." Light and darkness never mix. Only when you are walking with Jesus will you have light (understanding) in life. For He is truth, John 14:6.

Verse 16, Jesus' judgment is true, for He is not alone, but He and the Father, who sent Him, are together. He always does what the Father says. In (v.23-24), Jesus says, "You are from below, I am from above, you are of this world, I am not of this world. ......unless you believe that I am He, you shall die in your sins." These are truths that you must believe to be a disciple of Jesus. These truths and others like it will renew your mind and change your life.

Hebrews 8,9,10, gives us a view on what happened at the crucifixion and resurrection from God's prospective. Jesus, our High Priest took His own Blood (9:11-12), not the blood of goats and bulls but His own, into heaven itself (9:24). He put away sin by the sacrifice of Himself (9:26). He having offered this one sacrifice for sins for all time (10:12) sat down at the right hand of God. For by one offering He has perfected for all times those who are sanctified (10:14). We now can have confidence to enter the Holy Place by the blood of Jesus. By a new and living way which He inaugurated for us through the veil, His flesh (10:19-20). We have a High priest over the house of God.

The Promise: freedom, as you know the truth! (v.32)

The Condition: abiding in His Word, the Bible. Know your way around in it. Become a disciple, and go make disciples.

Take time to memorize the verse. Write it on a card, carry it with you, repeat it many times a day.
Also memorize the reference. Read the entire chapter of John 8, every day this week.
Let the word become flesh - a part of you!

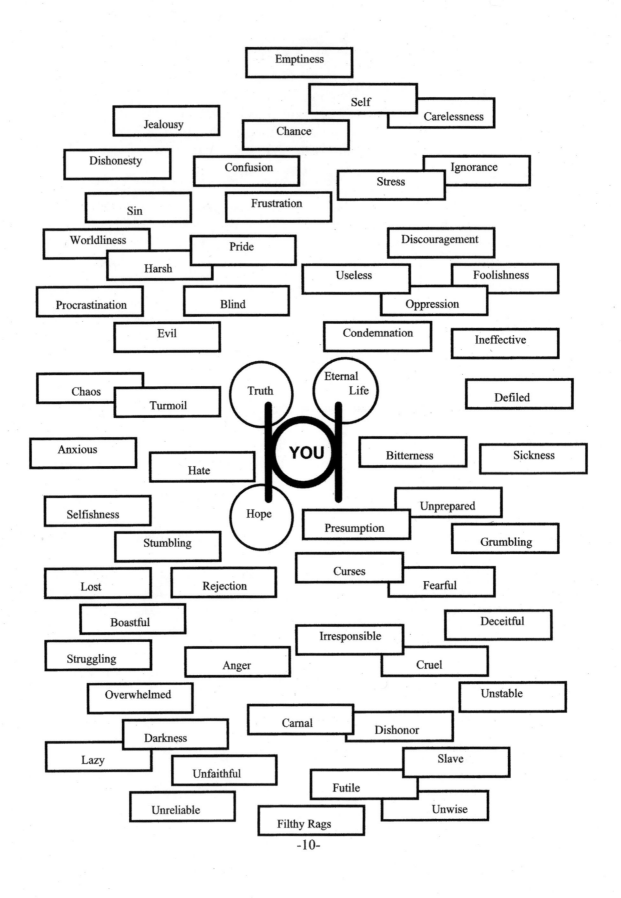

Hope

.... **Which is Christ in you**
the Hope of Glory
Colossians 1:27b

I in Christ, prepares Me for Heaven.
Christ in me, prepares me for earth.
I in Christ, I can face the Father.
Christ in Me, I can face the devil.

Hope comes from what we think, it is anchored in the mind, and gives us an expectancy for the future. Christ in you is your hope which means what was said before. All of chapter one is why Christ is your hope. Romans 5:5, "hope does not disappoint, because the love of God has been poured out within our hearts through the Holy Spirit. Verse 2 of Romans 5 states that hope is the glory of God.

Jesus Christ is the Son of God, who was with the Father in heaven forever, long before the beginning of time. He was with the Father when the world was created. For it was by Him that all things were created. He is the Word, He was with God, John 1. God said, and it was so, the world was created. God spoke. Jesus was that Word. (Col.1:17), He now holds the world together.

This same Jesus was born a man, first-born of all creation, (v.15). He was born a man so that He could take your sin and my sin upon Himself and pay the price of sin and death, (Romans 6:23). He not only died for sin, but He died to sin. In Him we can be dead to sin, Romans 6.

He arose from the dead. He is the first-born from the dead, (v.18). He is now the head of the church. He is our Lord and King. He has gone before us in all things. In Him we can come before the throne of grace, holy and blameless and beyond reproach (v. 22). The glory is hope, think about it. Christ in you, the hope of glory. Glory is what Adam and Eve lost when they sinned. They had been clothed in glory. This glory, this hope we have, as our minds are on Him who took our place, Jesus Christ, the Lord.

The Promise: hope: a positive outlook of the future

The Condition: The condition comes in Col.2, verses six and seven. As you therefore received Christ Jesus the Lord, <u>so walk in Him</u>. Having been firmly rooted and now <u>being built up in Him</u> and <u>established</u> in your faith just as you were <u>instructed</u> and <u>overflowing with gratitude</u>.

Take time to memorize the verse. Write it on a card, carry it with you, repeat it many times a day. Also memorize the reference. Read the entire chapter of Colossians 1, every day this week.
Let the word become flesh - a part of you!

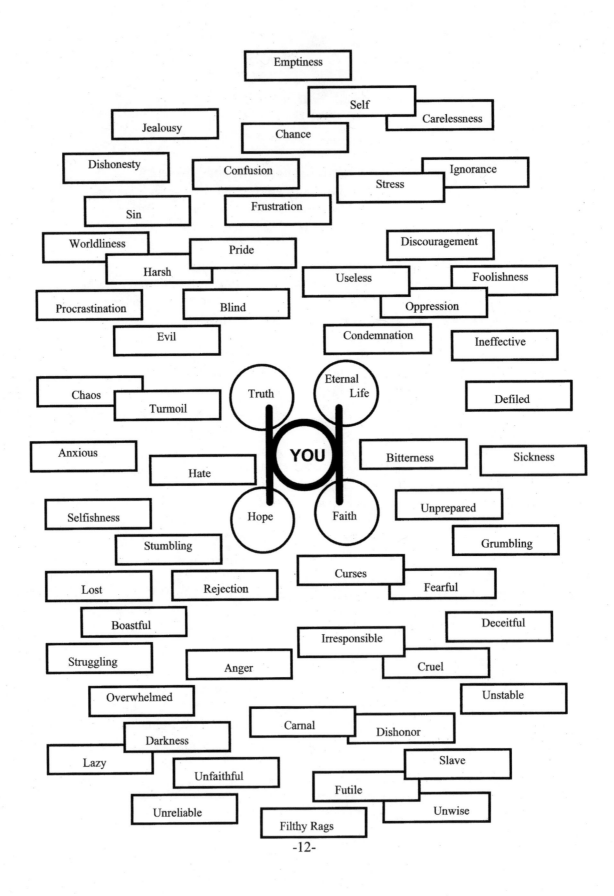

Faith

**So Faith comes from hearing,
and hearing by the Word of Christ.
Romans 10:17**

"Faith is: the assurance of things hoped for, the conviction of things not seen. It was by faith that men of long ago gained approval of God. It is by faith that we understand that the world was made by the Word of God, and that which is seen was not made out of things which are seen," Hebrews 11:1-3. The best explanation of faith comes from Luke 1:37-38. It says; "For nothing will be impossible with God. And Mary said, 'Behold, the bondslave of the Lord; be it done to me according to your word.' And the angel departed from her." This is truly a surrendered heart before God.

Faith comes by hearing. It is when we hear something and we are interested in what has been said. We have a desire to receive and understand the message presented. When we meditate on it, linger on the thought, this creates faith in our hearts. It is a process of thought. There is time involved here, for faith is a matter of the heart. Hearing comes to the mind, then proceeds to the heart, becoming faith.

True faith always originates directly in God's Word, it is always directly related to God's Word. It is anchored in the realm of the heart, which produces a definite change in those who profess it. When faith is in the heart "to believe" becomes an active verb. Because you "believe" you will then act on what you understand. It will give you a desire to understand even more. It will change your habits, character and your complete life.

Faith was reckoned to Abraham as righteousness. He believed God, after hearing the promise. He didn't assess his body and Sarah's womb, "but (Ro.4:20) with respect to the promise of God, he did not waver in unbelief, but grew strong in faith, and giving glory to God." He believed that God could do what He promised. This was reckoned to him as righteousness.

This is how it works - first we must hear (become interested and desire to understand). This then brings hope in our lives (hope is in our mind). As we meditate on the Word received, it becomes faith. True faith is in the heart. The result of this is righteousness. We act according to what is in our heart. Hearing, believing, becoming righteous, then moving on that, this is how the just live by faith.

The Promise: faith, which comes by hearing

The Condition: hearing, the hearing of God's Word

Take time to memorize the verse. Write it on a card, carry it with you, repeat it many times a day. Also memorize the reference. Read the entire chapter of Romans 10, every day this week.
Let the word become flesh - a part of you!

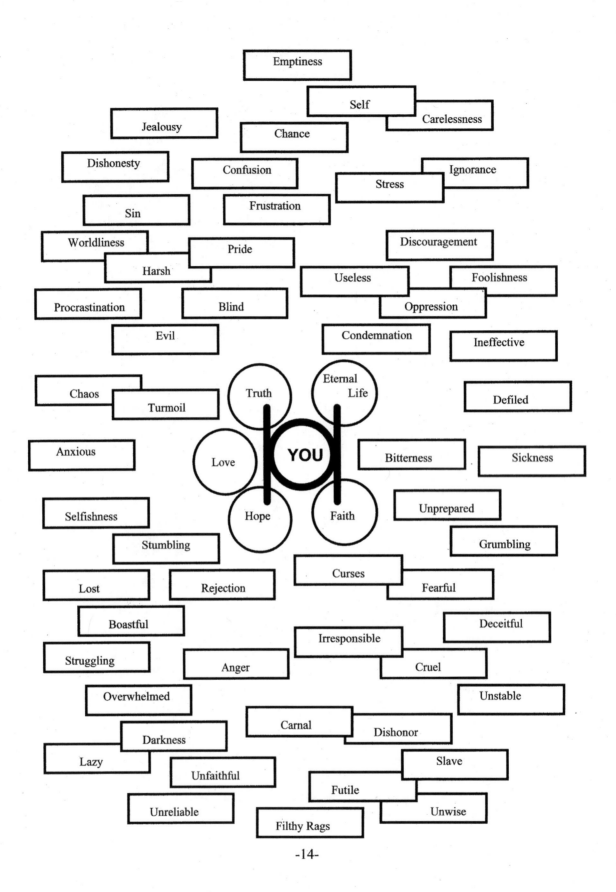

-14-

Love

**But now abide faith, hope, love,
these three;
but the greatest of these is love.
I Corinthians 13:13**

Without love all the good we do means nothing. It's an empty ritual. What is love? God is love, Although I Corinthians 13 tells us what love is, it's a picture of God.

And we could read it like this:
God is patient. God is kind. God is not jealous.
God does not brag. He is not arrogant.
God does not act unbecomingly.
He does not seek His own, nor is He provoked.
God does not take into account a wrong suffered.
He does not rejoice in unrighteousness, but He rejoices with the truth.
God bears all things. He believes all things.
He hopes all things. He endures all things.
God never fails.
For God is love, and the one who abides in love, abides in God, and God abides in Him, I John 4:16.
God wants good for you, His plans are for your best, not for evil. He wants you to have a future and a hope.

This is what this passage of Scripture is really saying;
God is patient with you. He's very kind, and He doesn't get jealous when you succeed.
God doesn't brag about what all He can do. He's not proud about it.
God doesn't act in ways that are difficult. He's always looking out for your good.
He truly is a good Father. He doesn't have to get back at anyone.
And did you know that He does suffer when He is wronged, but He doesn't keep track of that?
He is sad when you are in unrighteousness, but rejoices when you walk in truth.
God bears you up. He believes in you. He hopes for you. He endures all your short-comings.
God will not fail you. Nothing can separate us from the love of God, Romans 8:38-39.

The Promise: the good you do will have an eternal affect

The Condition: let the love of God flow through you

Take time to memorize the verse. Write it on a card, carry it with you, repeat it many times a day. Also memorize the reference. Read the entire chapter of I Corinthians 13, every day this week.
Let the word become flesh - a part of you!

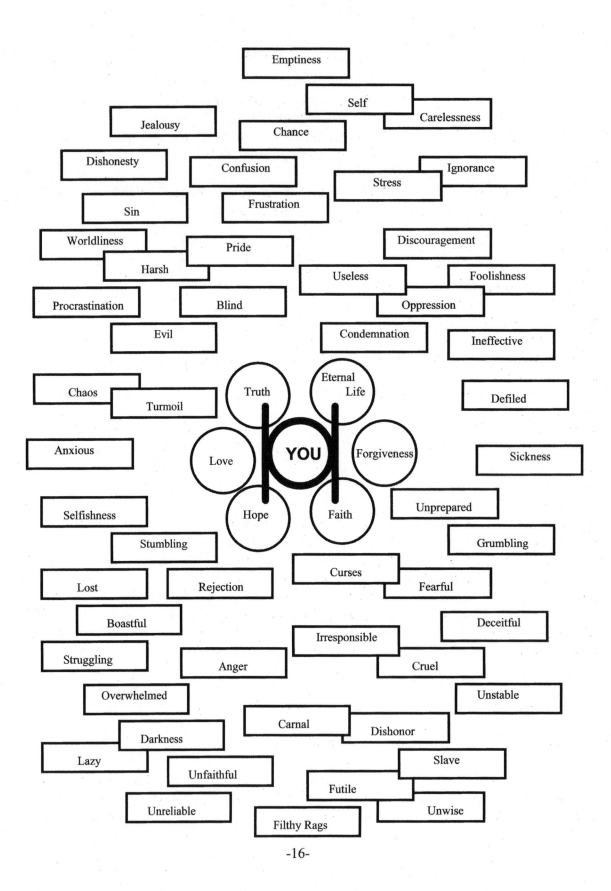

Forgiveness

Lord, how often shall
My brother sin against me
And I forgive him?
Matthew 18:21

Peter asked the Lord, how often do I need to forgive my brother? Matthew 18:21. His answer was seventy times seven. That's four hundred ninety times. He then gave us a story of a servant who was forgiven a great debt, and how he did not forgive as he was forgiven. His master handed him over to the torturers until he was able to repay all that he owed him. "So shall My heavenly Father also do to you, if each of you does not forgive his brother from your heart."(v.35)

Many Christians are miserable people, and this is the reason. They are not forgiving as they have been forgiven. This is the work of the Cross. Sin had to be dealt with. Sin has been dealt with. Jesus Christ took our sin, and because of sin, He died to that sin and for that sin, and we are forgiven. The debt you and I owed was more than we could ever pay. Jesus paid our debt.

Let this fact soak into your deepest inner being, that your sin was so great toward God there was no way you could pay it. It will make you forever grateful to your Savior. Take time to read the story in Matthew 18:21-35. The power of God in us, is power enough to forgive others. God never asked us to do anything but that He also provides the means to do it. If He is asking us to forgive 490 times, we are able to do that with His help, I Corinthians 10:13.

Forgiveness is a decision. The working out of that decision can be painful. Decide to forgive your brother, your sister. Tell God about it. You might not feel like you have forgiven at all. For whatever it is might still hurt. Do not back away from your decision. If it wants to come back, say I have forgiven, and let God bring healing to your life. Re-forgive every morning and sincerely ask for a healing. Even situations that are so difficult you might not think you can ever be healed, God is able and willing. Many times this will take some time. Let God's power work in you. It is not always easy.

Christ made a decision to come to earth and give his life, so that mankind can be forgiven, Philippians 2:5-8. But as a man, in Luke 22:44, He cried so hard that drops of blood fell as sweat to the earth.

The Promise: you will be perfect, as your Father in heaven is perfect, Matthew 5:48

The Condition: a heart attitude, a desire to walk before God blameless and pure

Take time to memorize the verse. Write it on a card, carry it with you, repeat it many times a day. Also memorize the reference. Read the entire chapter of Matthew 18, every day this week.
Let the word become flesh - a part of you!

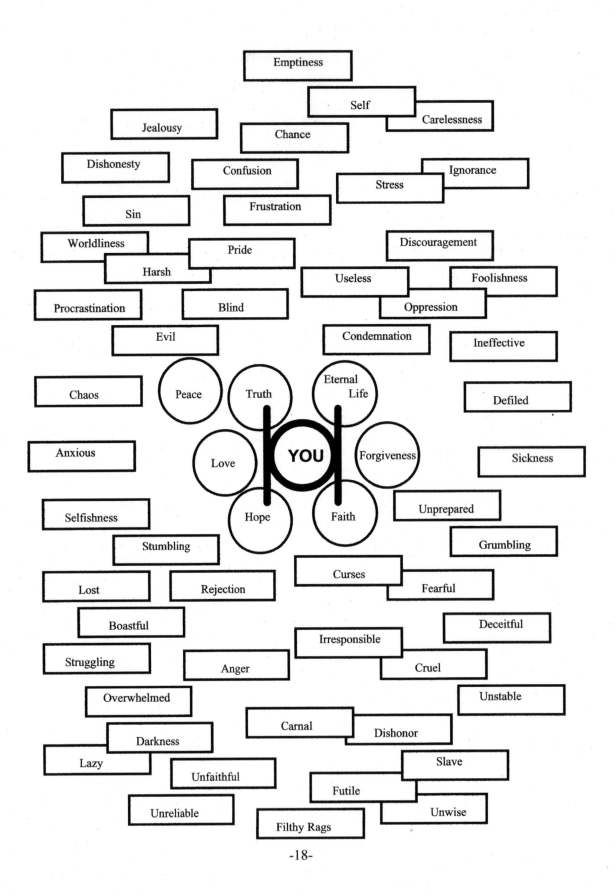

-18-

Peace

..... Let him seek peace
and pursue it
I Peter 3:11b

Love, joy, peace, are fruits of the Spirit, Galatians 5:22. Peace is the heart cry of every person. It is found when we seek it, when we pursue it. Romans 14:19, "let us pursue the things which make for peace and the building up of one another."

The issue is, do we want peace more than we want our own way. This passage of scripture really begins at chapter two, verse eleven, where Peter urges us to abstain from fleshly lusts. For our flesh wages war against the soul. He then goes on to explain to us, how to submit to every human institution, (v.3). Whether it is the king, a governor, a master (boss), a husband, or a wife. If we all could understand and desire to submit properly to the proper authority of one another, we would have a perfectly peaceful world. Christ Jesus left an example for us to follow (2:22-25). "He Himself (Jesus) bore our sins in His body on the Cross, that we might die to sin and live to righteousness." This brings us peace of heart, peace with God.

If you want to love life and see good days, in other words, enjoy life, this is the way you do it. You refrain your tongue from evil, your lips from speaking guile (deceit), turn away from evil and do good. After this then you seek peace, and then pursue peace. When you pursue something you don't quit until you have it.

Romans 14 speaks of the things of peace and the building up of one another, peace with one another. We are called for this very purpose. The things of peace are mentioned in I Peter 3:8-9.
They are being: 1) harmonious (agreeable), 2) sympathetic (sharing each others struggles),
3) brotherly (doing things for the good of all), 4) kindhearted (remember, you have been forgiven),
5) humble in spirit (esteeming the other person higher than yourself even when they are wrong).
6) Not returning evil for evil, or insulting for insult, but giving a blessing instead.
This is peace with mankind. The more you can attain these two, peace with God and peace with mankind, the more you have peace within yourself. It is when you are at peace that you are able to hear what the Holy Spirit is speaking to you.

The Promise: peace, "you were called for the very purpose that you might inherit a blessing."

The Condition: to desire peace more, then the lusts within you, submitting to those in authority.

Take time to memorize the verse. Write it on a card, carry it with you, repeat it many times a day. Also memorize the reference. Read from I Peter 2:11 through I Peter 3, every day this week.
Let the word become flesh - a part of you!

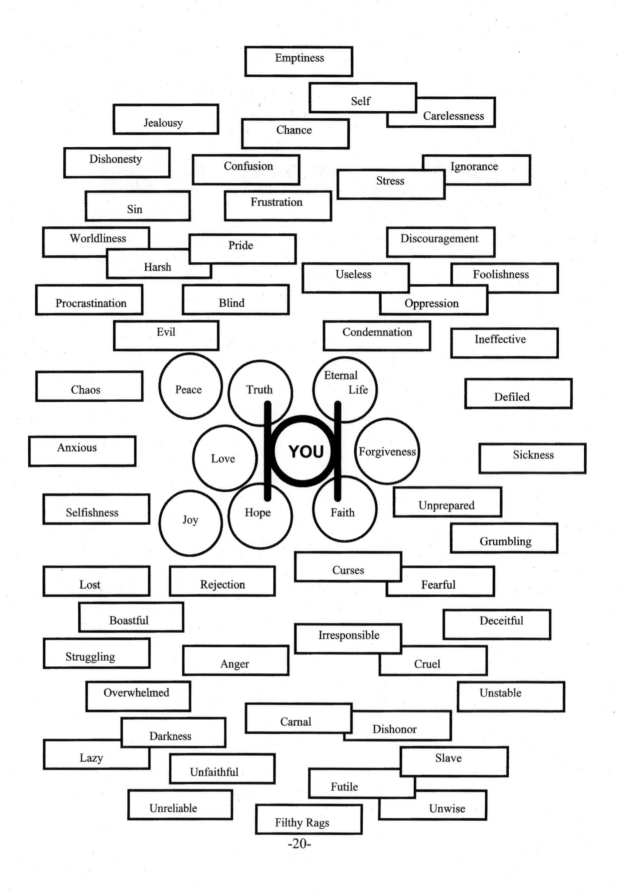

-20-

Joy

**Until now you have asked for nothing
in My name;
ask, and you will receive,
that your joy may be made full.
John 16:24**

In John 13, Jesus and His disciples had the last Supper. It was their last time before He would be crucified. John chapter 14, 15, and 16 are His last words to them. In John 17, He prayed. Read all of these four chapters this week. Sit at Jesus feet. For He had all of us in His mind when He was sharing and praying this last evening that He walked on earth as a man. In chapter 17 verse 20, He confirms this. "I do not ask in behalf of these alone, but for those also who believe in Me through their word.

Jesus starts chapter 16, by saying, he has spoken these things to us that we may be kept from stumbling. He ends the chapter saying, He has spoken these things that in Him, we may have peace. "In the world, you have tribulation, but take courage, I have overcome the world."

Joy comes from knowing that we can talk to the Father about whatever our needs are, and that He will move on our behalf. As you read through this chapter it is plain to understand, that not everything will always be easy in this walk with the Lord. But as He explains that He is leaving, He also explains that He will send the Helper, (v.7), the Spirit of Truth, (v.13). He (Holy Spirit) will guide us into all truth. He reveals the Father's will to us.

It's not so much what comes our way, it's how we deal with the situations that makes the difference. In every trial there is a benefit for you. Look for the benefit. God, the Father has allowed it to come about, because it will conform you to be more like Jesus.

When you face something hard. First, know that these things have passed through the hands of a loving Father. Second, ask yourself, how do I respond to this situation that I can come out a better person. Third, take it all to God the Father in prayer. Fourth, expect an answer and rejoice in it. It might not be exactly the way you thought it would be. But you can be sure it is the best for you.

The Promise: As our prayers are answered, our joy is full.

The Condition: to come to the Father, in the Name of Jesus, with all our needs. He wants us to talk to Him about every concern we have. Nothing is too small, neither is anything too big.

Take time to memorize the verse. Write it on a card, carry it with you, repeat it many times a day. Also memorize the reference. Read chapters 13,14,15,16,17 of John, this week.
Let the word become flesh - a part of you!

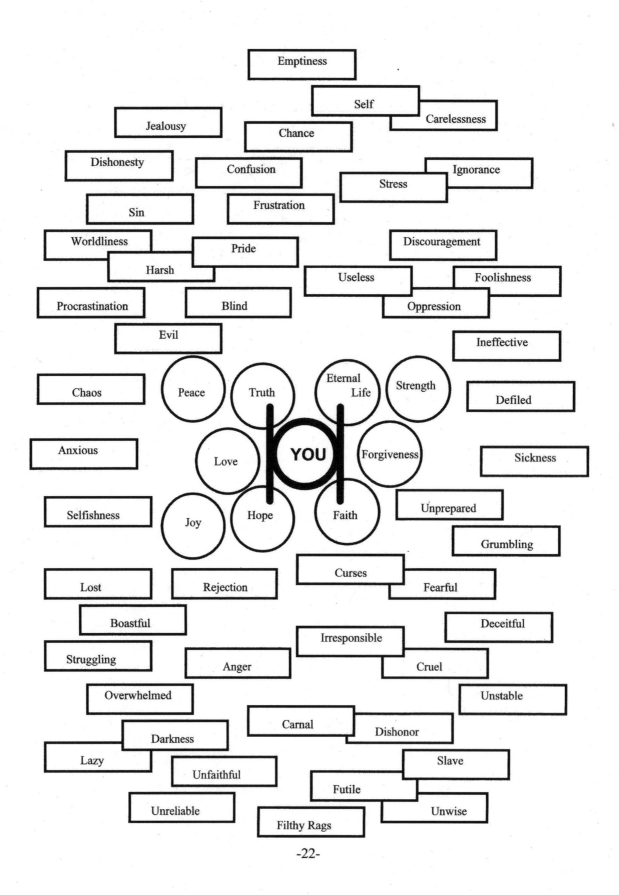

Strength

**Do not be grieved,
for the joy of the Lord
is your strength
Nehemiah 8:10b**

Nehemiah the governor (king), and Ezra the priest and scribe, and the Levities, who taught the people, were speaking to the people, explaining to them how to respond to the Word of God. In the beginning of the chapter we read, how they have gathered together to read the Word. The people were responding to the Word by weeping and mourning over it. They saw all the things they had missed. No, he says, don't weep, for this day is holy to the Lord. In verse 10, he continued, Go, eat the fat, drink of the sweet, and send portions to him who has nothing prepared.

How does this apply to you and me? This is all about how we read the Word of God. We all are kings and priests, Revelation 1:6. Jesus brought this all together when He paid the price for sin. I John 2:27 "And as for you, the anointing which you received from Him abides in you, and you have no need for anyone to teach you, but as His anointing teaches you about all things, and is true and is not a lie, and just as it has taught you, you abide in Him." After Jesus went to heaven, He send the Holy Spirit to earth to teach us, as we read the Word of God.

This is how we are to eat the Word. Back to Nehemiah 8:10 now. He said, Go, eat the fat, (see the extras, the good for yourself) drink the sweet (drink it in, drink in the promises) and send portions to him who has nothing prepared (share with them who are discouraged).

For you see, the time you spent reading the Word of God is holy, holy to the Lord. Remember that, when you sit down to read the Word, God is smiling on you. The Holy Spirit is there, He will teach you all things. It is a holy moment. Don't let the devil come and condemn you, but look for the promises, drink it in, let the Holy Spirit teach you, and receive understanding. Rejoice in the Word.

The Promise: you will be strengthened

The Condition: Rejoice in the Word. Resist the enemy. Do not let him condemn you. Let the Holy Spirit teach you - look for promises. Remember, the Word of God is a love letter to you. Share it with those around you.

Take time to memorize the verse. Write it on a card, carry it with you, repeat it many times a day. Also memorize the reference. Read the entire chapter of Nehemiah 8, every day this week.
Let the word become flesh - a part of you!

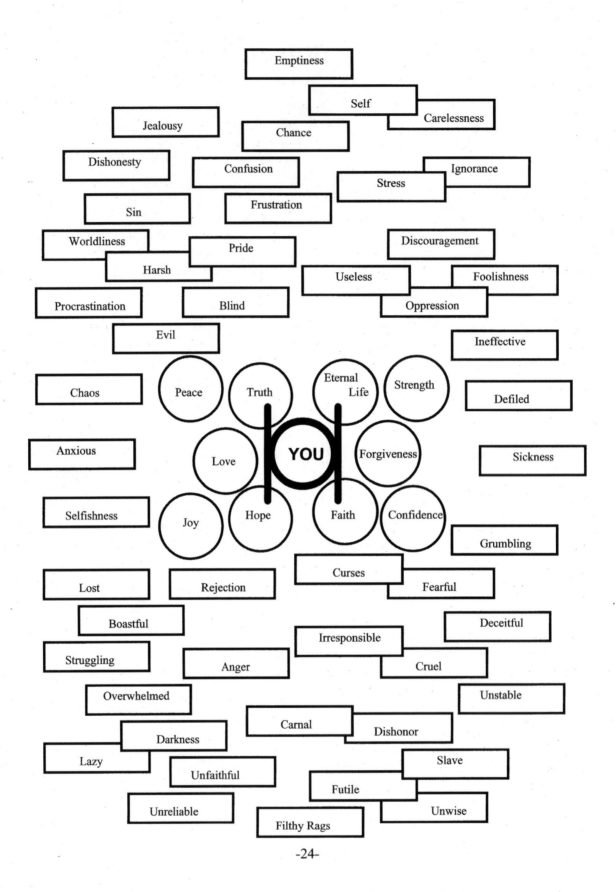

-24-

Confidence

**Wherefore take up the whole armor of God,
that ye may be able
to resist in the evil day,
And having done everything, to stand firm.
Ephesians 6:13**

1) having girded your loins with Truth
2) having put on the breastplate of Righteousness
3) having shod your feet with the preparation of the Gospel of Peace
4) taking up the shield of Faith
5) take the Helmet of Salvation
6) the Sword of the Spirit, which is the Word of God
7) with all Prayer and Petition - pray at all times
I in Christ, prepares Me for Heaven. Christ in me, prepares me for earth.
I in Christ, I can face the Father. Christ in me, I can face the devil.

Verse ten - Finally, (after all of Ephesians) be strong in the Lord. It is in the Lord that we are strong.
Chapter One, Paul talks about the inheritance we have in Christ (v.7).
Chapter Two, we are raised up with Him and seated with Him in heavenly Places (v.6).
Chapter Three, we are to carry out the Eternal Purpose in Christ Jesus our Lord, because in Him we have boldness and confidence access through faith in Him (v.9-12).
Chapter Four, he shared that Christ has given us grace and gifts, that the body of Christ might become a mature body, according to the measure of the statue - which belongs to the fullness of Christ. In other words - conformed to Christ.
Chapter Five, continues on with practical application and at the end He shows us how that a marriage is like what Christ and the church are.
Then in verse ten of chapter six, He says, finally now, be strong in the Lord. How? He has made the way. The Devil has a plan against you. God has prepared for us an armor that he cannot overthrow. Take up this armor, and be on the alert, v.18. The battle is done in prayer, but we can be confident. It is in the Lord that we are strong, in the strength of His might, dressed in Him.

The Promise: being able to resist in the evil day, after everything is done, to still stand.

The Condition: letting go of self, looking to Christ, being in Him, Him being in you, putting on the armor of God, being prepared to meet each day.

Take time to memorize the verse. Write it on a card, carry it with you, repeat it many times a day.
Also memorize the reference. Read the entire chapter of Ephesians 6, every day this week.
Let the word become flesh - a part of you!

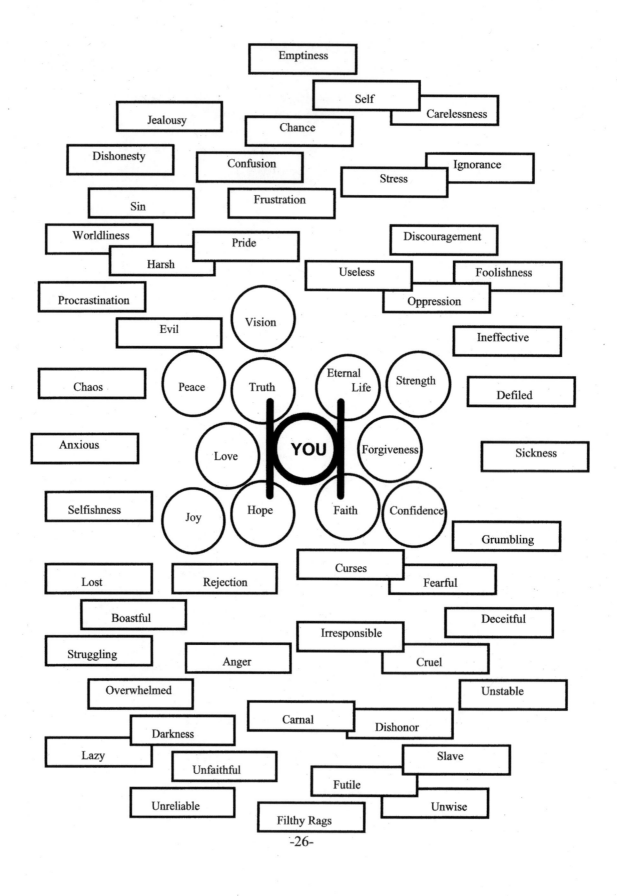

-26-

Vision

Where there is no vision,
the people are unrestrained.
But happy is he,
who keeps the Law.
Proverbs 29:18

In order to solve a problem, you must have a vision, a working idea, a plan. It will restrain you from doing anything that will hinder the vision. This is the driving force of your life, be it good or bad.

You need a vision for your lifetime, a vision for each year, a vision for each day. A vision of why God placed you on earth at this time. God is not asking you to do anything you cannot do.

At the end of our lives we would want to hear God say, "Well done, good and faithful servant." This would mean that we have accomplished His plan for our lives. How do we get there? Luke 16:10, "He who is faithful in a very little thing is faithful also in much; and he who is unrighteous in a very little thing is unrighteous also in much."

A day is a small thing in your lifetime. God has a vision and a purpose for each day of your life. As you read and pray each morning ask God what His vision is for you that day. In every situation that comes your way, God has a plan. Stop and ask God, "What would you have me do here?" Be in tune with God. And it will help you to see the vision for each year. Finally the vision for your lifetime.

Ask yourself three questions
   1) What is God's Plan for my life?
   2) What is the Devil's Plan for my life?
   3) Which do I want to fulfill?

God has a plan for each day of our lives. This is why it is so important to spend time with Him before you start your day. His plan is not more than you can accomplish. Take your plan before Him, and let Him rearrange it.

The Promise: becoming a person who is self-discipline (restrained) and happy

The Condition: having a vision, seeing, understanding what God's plan is and using self-control and perseverance to accomplish it. (Many times we want to do more then what God has called us to do.)

Take time to memorize the verse. Write it on a card, carry it with you, repeat it many times a day. Also memorize the reference. Read the entire chapter of Proverbs 29, every day this week..
Let the word become flesh - a part of you!

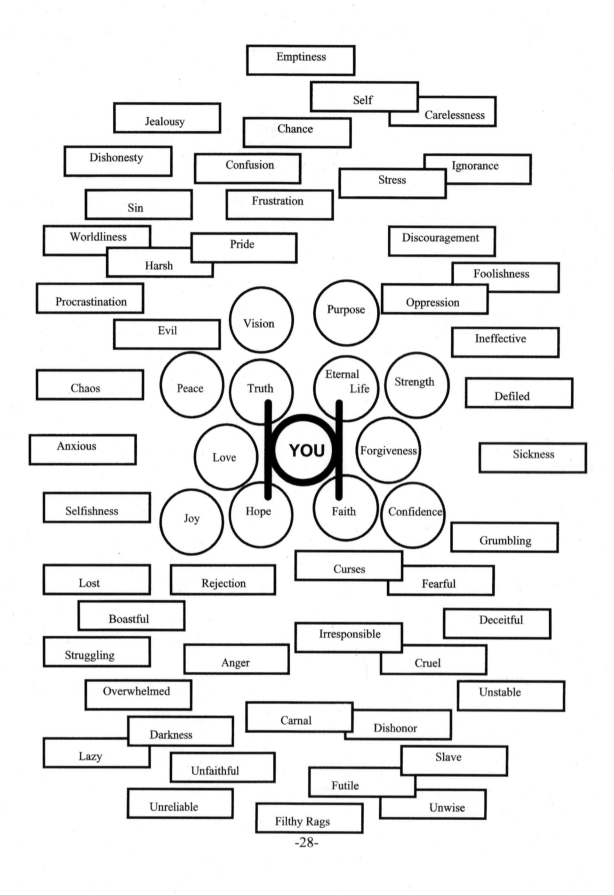

Purpose

**And we know
that God causes all things
to work together for good,
to those who love God,
to those who are called
according to His purpose.
Romans 8:28**

Purpose in life is the difference between being successful in life and not. If you find yourself with feeling like you have no purpose, it is a vision that you need first. Even if you start off with the wrong vision, God can then direct you in the right way.

"God causes all things to work together for good, to those who are called according to His purpose." His purpose is that we are conformed to the image (likeness) of His Son. He uses the rest of the chapter to explain what that would mean. He predestined, and called you to become like Jesus. Then He justified you (just-as-if-you-had-never-sinned) and glorified you (glory is the presence of God). He is for you. He gave His Son, so that He can give you all things. No one can bring a charge against you. Jesus is interceding for you. Nothing can separate you from the love of Christ, nor the love of God. Verse thirty-seven says, "But in all things we overwhelmingly conquer through Him, who loved us." This is God's purpose for you.

Chapter 8 starts out saying, "There is therefore no condemnation for those who are in Christ Jesus." God has condemned sin in the flesh, for He send His Son in the likeness of sinful flesh, being an offering for sin. By walking in the Spirit, we can have a mindset of life and peace. For the Spirit of God dwells in us, putting to death the deeds (sins) of the body. We are made alive to God, in Christ Jesus. This is His purpose for us, this is how we become conformed into the likeness of Jesus. When His purpose becomes your purpose, that is when grace will really flow. Purpose in your heart to become like Jesus. At times what comes our way does not feel good, but when we look for the good in it, it will make us more like Jesus.

The Promise: you will become conformed to the image of Christ

The Condition: being in Christ Jesus, walking according to the Spirit, having a mindset on the Spirit, which is life and peace.

With two blessings going ahead of you, you are beginning to feel a little more protected.

Take time to memorize the verse. Write it on a card, carry it with you, repeat it many times a day. Also memorize the reference. Read the entire chapter of Romans 8, every day this week..
Let the word become flesh - a part of you!

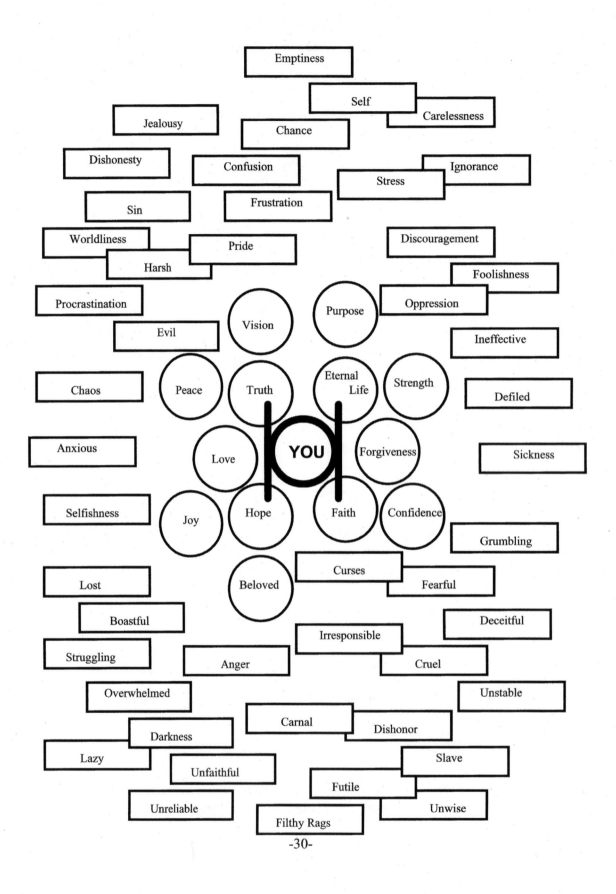

-30-

Beloved

I am my Beloved's and my Beloved is mine
Song of Solomon 6:3a
He has brought me to His banqueting table
And His banner over me is Love.
Song of Solomon 2:4b

Song of Solomon was written by Solomon. It is written as a dialogue with three persons speaking, the groom, the bride, and the daughters of Jerusalem, mostly the groom and the bride. The lines we used here were those of the bride expressing her confidence in His love for her.

Instead of studying just one chapter, read through the whole book of Song of Solomon. It is a picture of a man and a woman in love, showing us the love that Christ has for us, His bride. Do you run after His love? Chapter 1:4, "draw me after you and let us run together," the bride speaking to her lover.

Are you in love with Jesus? Do you know that He is in love with you? Chapter 4 verse 9, this is the groom (Jesus) speaking to the Bride (you)" You have made my heart beat faster, my sister, my bride; You have made my heart beat faster with a single glance of your eyes,"
   Jesus loves you. Remember, the song we learned as children;
"Yes, Jesus loves me. Yes, Jesus loves me.   Yes, Jesus loves me. The Bible tells me so."
This song is not for children only, but for all of God's children.

Now read Ephesians 5:22-33. Marriage is a time where two people in love bring their things together and they say, " What is mine is yours, and what is yours is mine." This is the longing of Jesus' heart. Not only that you would give Him all of you, but that you receive all of His. It is a covenant relationship where nothing is withheld from the other. Why did He do it? Why was He willing? Love in His heart for you, for me, that's why. I John 4:10

The Promise: you will know that you are one with Jesus, that you are His, and He is yours.

The Condition: Understanding the exchange at the Cross:
 He was: 1) punished, that we might be forgiven; 2) wounded, that we might be healed;
3) made sin with our sinfulness, that we might be made righteous with His righteousness;
4) died our death, that we might receive life; 5) made a curse, that we might enter into the blessing;
6) endured our poverty, that we might have His abundance; 7) bore our shame, that we share His glory;
8) endured our rejection, that we might have His acceptance with the Father;
9) was cut off by death, that we might have life and be joined to God eternally.

Take time to memorize the verse. Write it on a card, carry it with you, repeat it many times a day.
Also memorize the reference. Read through Song of Solomon; Ephesians 5:22-33; and I John.
Let the word become flesh - a part of you!

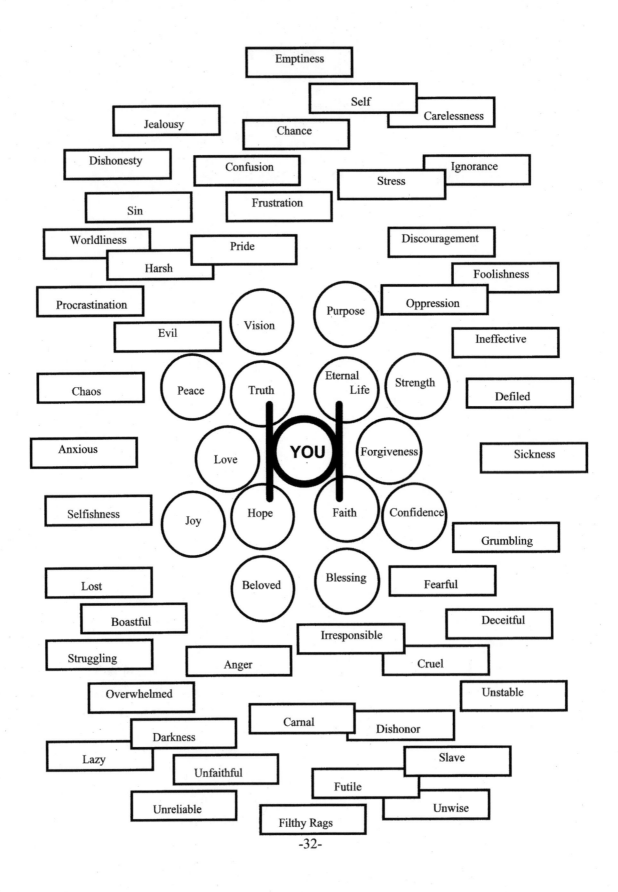

Blessing

Blessed be the God and Father
of our Lord Jesus Christ,
who has blessed us
with every spiritual blessing
in the heavenly places
in Christ.
Ephesians 1:3

God has blessed us with every spiritual blessing. In Christ we have life and life more abundant. Do you know that God had already chosen you before the foundation of the world. Before He made light or separated the waters. He adopted you as sons and daughters. It's all through Jesus Christ, for in Him we have redemption. He gave His life, He shed His blood, that we might be forgiven. What a blessing!

He worked it all out, that we can receive an inheritance with Christ. He gave the Holy Spirit as a pledge to that inheritance. In this book we are studying about sixty blessings. There are so many, many more. I hope when you come to the end, that you will not want to stop, but will go on finding blessings in the Word. Try to find one even this week that is not mentioned in this study.

God, the Father is such a loving Father. He made us parents, mothers and fathers, to help us to understand His great love for us. The love that parents have for their children causes them to make many sacrifices in life, and do it joyfully. Children have a way of drawing something from the deepest parts of our being. As parents we want to always be there for them, help them in every way. We want success to be theirs. But we are limited in so many ways. The very best fathers and mothers run out of energy, they don't understand, they aren't there when needed. We all fail miserably. God never fails, He is unlimited. He is everything and more than we long to be. He is the Father of fathers.

You are now totally surrounded by Blessings, do you want to stop here, or go on and fortify yourself as Solomon did.

The Promise: abundant blessings,

The Condition: Pray Paul's prayer (vs.17-19) that the Father of glory would gave you a spirit of wisdom, a spirit of revelation in the knowledge of Him. Ask Him that the eyes of your heart would be enlightened, so that you may know; 1) the hope of His calling 2) the riches of His inheritance 3) the surpassing greatness of His power toward us - who believe.

Take time to memorize the verse. Write it on a card, carry it with you, repeat it many times a day. Also memorize the reference. Read through the entire chapter of Ephesians 1, every day this week.
Let the word become flesh - a part of you!

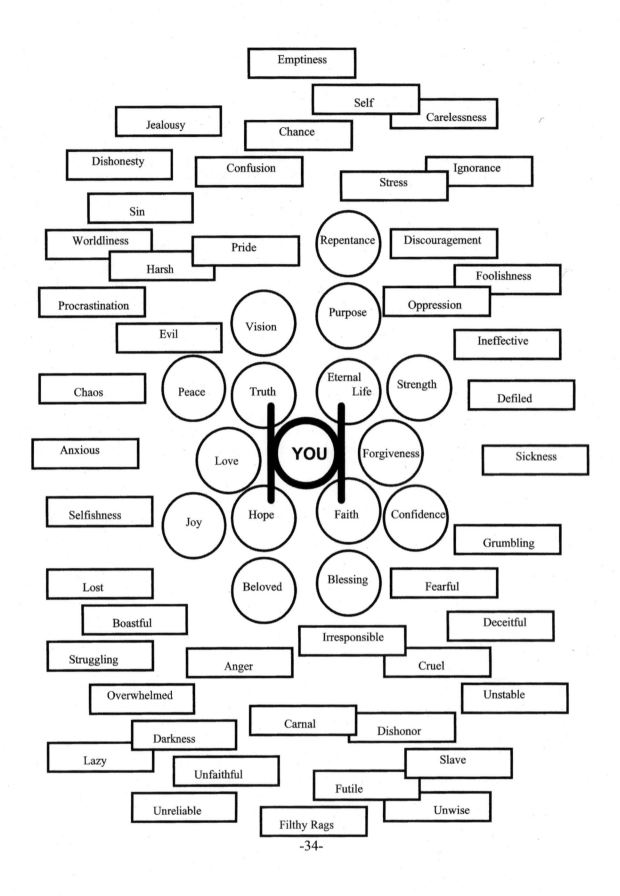

Repentance

Therefore,
gird your minds for action,
keep sober in spirit,
fix your hope completely on the grace
to be brought to you
at the revelation of Jesus Christ.
I Peter 1:13

True repentance is -- a firm, inward decision, a change of mind. It is an inner change of mind resulting in an outward turning, or turning around to move in a completely new direction. Every person born on earth is born going forward in the kingdom of Satan. As you acknowledge that and see your need of a Savior, this will point you toward the Father in heaven. This is the beginning of a repentant life.

Without true repentance there can be no true faith. Without such repentance, faith alone is an empty profession. The result of professing faith and not practicing true repentance is that we have neither the favor of God nor the respect of the world.

In Hebrews 6:1, Paul tells us that the first of the basic doctrines in Christian life is repenting from dead works. This is an ongoing process. Leading a life of repentance means always being ready to change where God is speaking to us. It is what brings grace and peace into our hearts. Each one of us can do this because Jesus came and made a way for us. He made a way, where there seemed to be no way.

As you are now pushing back the confusion in your life, you will want to be ready to hear from God, and as you hear Him, act upon it. Living a repentant lifestyle will bring you into a victorious life. Every person was born walking away from God. We were all headed toward hell. Living in a lifestyle of repentance is going forward, closer and closer to God. There is no standing still in the kingdom of God. We are either going forward or backward. When we backslid, where are we headed? It is the first blessing to start that double wall around you.

The Promise: grace and peace in our lives, v.2 and v.13. The grace to change (repent), turn around.

The Condition: gird (ready) your mind for action. Get a revelation of Jesus Christ. You were redeemed by the Blood of Jesus (v.18-19). The cost of our redemption was God's Son. He gave His life, His Blood, His body. The more one studies on these things, the more we want to change in any area we find our lives not being like Him. Study much on the Blood of Jesus. It will make repenting (change) in any area of your life much easier.

Take time to memorize the verse. Write it on a card, carry it with you, repeat it many times a day. Also memorize the reference. Read the entire chapter of I Peter 1, every day this week.
Let the word become flesh - a part of you!

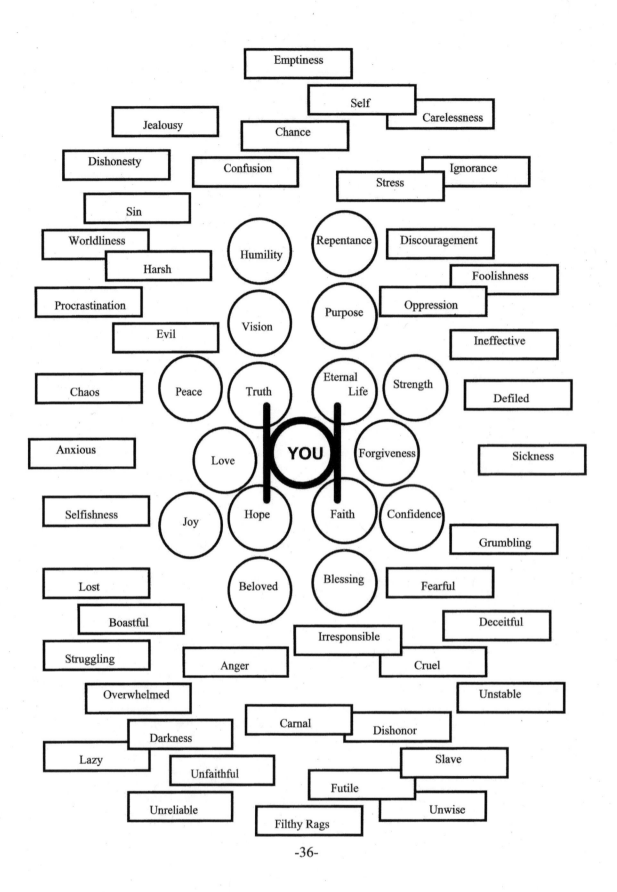

Humility

Humble yourselves, therefore,
under the mighty hand of God,
that He may exalt you at the proper time,
casting all your anxiety
upon Him,
because
He cares for you.
I Peter 5:6,7

Humility is when we totally depend on God. It is the first duty and the highest virtue of man. The root of it all. We need only look back to where everything came from, and know we owe it all to Him. Man's main care need be that we are before God as an empty vessel in which He can dwell and manifest His mighty power and goodness.

Clothing ourselves with humility: means putting on a mantle, a robe of humility, doing it God's way, not mine. This is a life of repentance. Humility is the key that unlocks the promises. It opens the way for you to meet the conditions as you go through this book. Only as you depend on God will this work in your life. It does not mean, letting every one walk all over you, but that you acquaint yourself with the Word and stand up for truth.

We again see grace here, how do we live a lifestyle of repentance and humility? It is through a life of prayer, which we will study next week. Humility, repentance and prayer bring grace into of our lives. Grace will be discussed in a later study.

Tidbits in living a humble life. Pray and Obey and Understand later.
His hand is a mighty hand. We don't always understand what He is doing or why He is doing it. To obey is to do it, immediately, thoroughly, and joyfully.
When you are wrong, admit it. When you are right, be fit to live with.

The Promise: in verse 10 - after you have suffered for a little while (resisting, standing firm, staying alert, are not always easy, it's suffering) then, the God of grace will Himself - perfect, confirm, strengthen and establish you.

The Condition: casting all your cares upon Him, remembering how much He cares for you. As you do, keep a sober spirit, be alert, resist the enemy firmly. Don't move.

Take time to memorize the verse. Write it on a card, carry it with you, repeat it many times a day.
Also memorize the reference. Read the entire chapter of I Peter 5, every day this week.
Let the Word become flesh - a part of you!

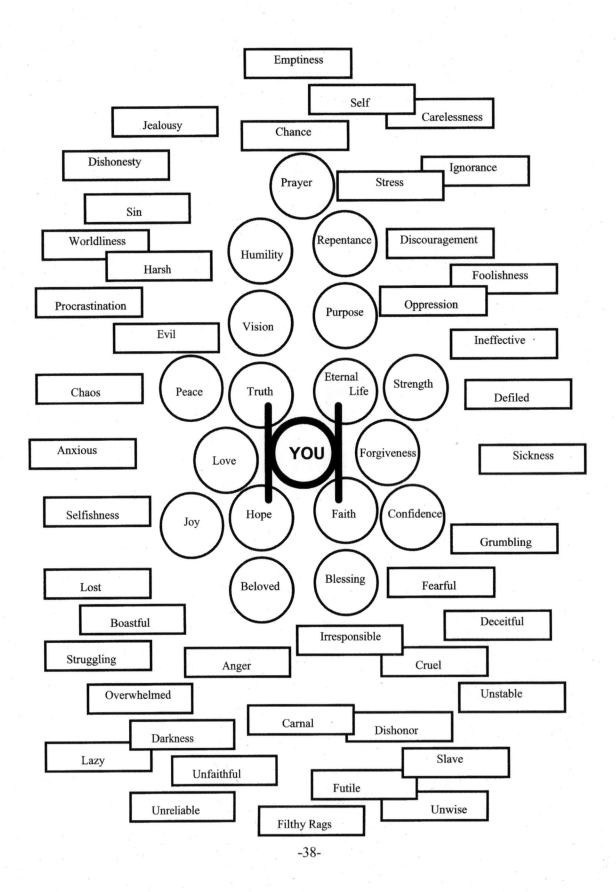

-38-

Prayer

**For there is one God
and one mediator also
between God and men,
the man Christ Jesus.
I Timothy 2:5**

This is prayer: coming to God the Father, through Jesus Christ, His Son, by the intercessions of the Holy Spirit. "And whatsoever ye shall ask in my name, that will I do, that the Father may be glorified in the Son." John 14:13

Prayer is communication between God the Father and mankind. He hears and answers prayer. Casting all our cares upon Him means: taking everything to Him in prayer. He wants to hear from you. He will talk to you. Jesus is our example. In the Gospels, we read many places where Jesus went alone or to the mountains to pray. He took time for God. His disciples asked Him to teach them to pray.

Come to the Father in worship and be thankful of His goodness to you. Thank and praise Him for the Blood, which is your redemption. Pray for His will in your life, your spouse, your children, your church and friends, your nation and around the world. Pray specific prayers, but always pray for yourself first. When you get the things on your heart settled, then you will find it easy to pray for others. This changed my prayer life when I understood this concept.

In I Thessalonians 5:17 he says, "pray without ceasing." This means all the time! How do we do this? When you get up early enough to spent time with God in the morning before you start your day, this then puts you in tune with God and into a humble attitude, where you can cast all your cares on Him all day long. And if you are willing to change where you need to and live a life of repentance, it will bring grace and peace into your life. It all goes together.

The Promise: you will be able to lead a tranquil and quiet life in all godliness and dignity, (verse 2). He goes on to tell us - this is good and acceptable in the sight of God our Savior.

The Condition: to come to God the Father, through Jesus Christ. God is a holy God. In Jesus Christ we are then holy and free from sin. This is the only way we can come to God, the Father, in Christ Jesus our Lord.

Now that you have five blessings walking before you, let's add a couple at your rear guard.

Take time to memorize the verse. Write it on a card, carry it with you, repeat it many times a day. Also memorize the reference. Read the entire chapter of I Timothy 2, every day this week.
Let the word become flesh - a part of you!

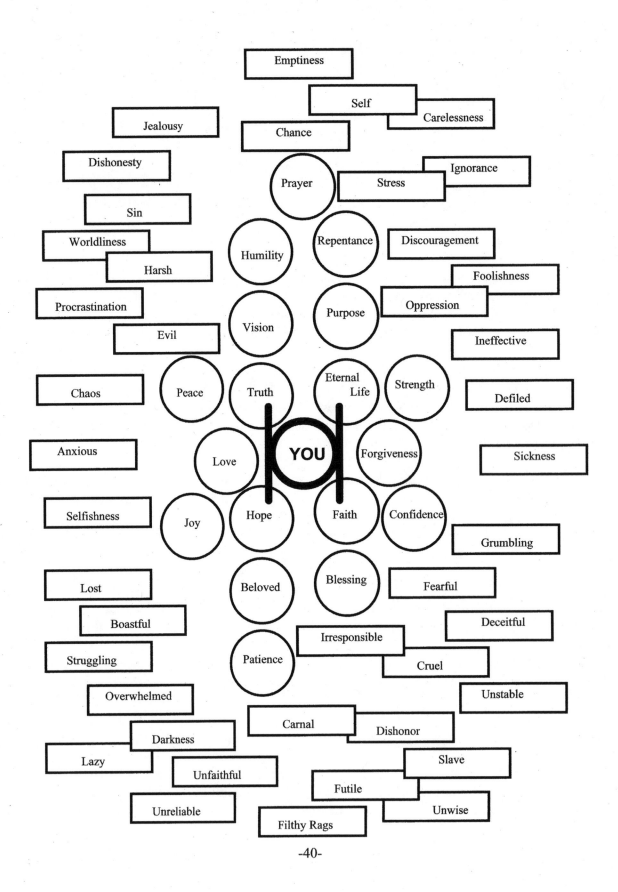

-40-

Patience

But the Fruit of the Spirit is
Love, Joy, Peace
Patience, Kindness, Goodness
Faithfulness, Gentleness, Self-Control
against such things there are no law.
Galatians 5:22,23

Fruit is what we harvest when a crop is completed. It makes a difference how we take care of our garden as to how much fruit we receive. Patience is only one of the fruits of the Spirit. We will be studying the others at different places. In verse 24, those who belong to Christ Jesus have crucified the flesh with its passions and desires. Being impatient is a desire of the flesh. It is a choice we make. I will be patient or I will be impatient. Patience means: capable of bearing affliction with calmness, tolerant, and understanding.

Since patience is a fruit, a fruit (result) of walking in the Spirit, then we need to walk by the Spirit. (For if you walk by the Spirit, you will not carry out the desire of the flesh (v.16). Fruit is the result of cultivating the Spirit. When we desire to have green beans, we plant green beans. We then take care of the green bean plants. We cultivate them, keep them bug free, make sure they have moist soil to grow in. The harvest (fruit) is green beans. So it is with the fruit of the Spirit. As you live by the Spirit, and you also walk by the Spirit, you will find the fruit appearing. You now have a choice whether to pick it or not. Walking by the Spirit is faith working through love. We, through the Spirit, by faith (faith in the Spirit) are waiting for the hope of righteousness (v.5-6). "You were called to freedom" (v.13) "through love serve one another." Verse 14, "You shall love your neighbor as yourself." Being led by the Spirit will keep you from fulfilling the desires of your flesh. It really is a choice.

Being sensitive to the Holy Spirit is how you walk by the Spirit. If you are praying and reading daily, and have a mindset on the Spirit, then when you are faced with a difficult situation the first thought that will come to your mind is most often from the Spirit. The second thought will be your mind telling you why the first thought would not work.

The Promise: freedom, (it was for freedom that Christ set us free) you will be able to serve others and love doing it.

The Condition: crucifying the flesh, its passions and desires, living by grace, believing that the Holy Spirit is well able to lead you.

Take time to memorize the verse. Write it on a card, carry it with you, repeat it many times a day. Also memorize the reference. Read the entire chapter of Galatians 5, every day this week.
Let the word become flesh - a part of you!

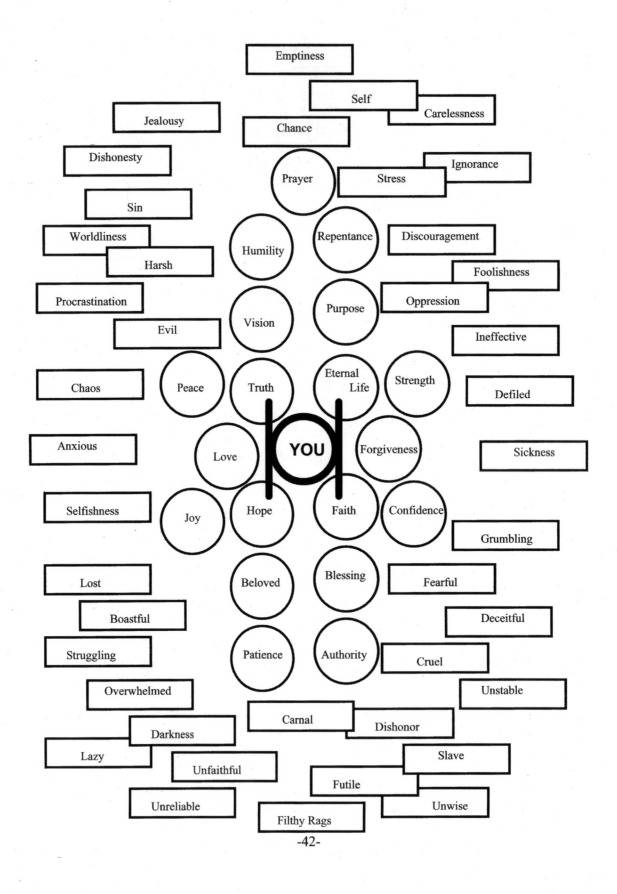

Authority

Jesus came to them and spoke unto them, saying,
All authority hath been given unto Me
in heaven and on earth.
Go therefore, and make disciples
of all the nations, baptizing them into the name
of the Father
and of the Son
and of the Holy Spirit:
teaching them to observe all that I commanded you:
and lo, I am with you always, even unto the end of the world.
Matthew 28:18-20

Understanding authority is the key to having authority. The centurion in Matthew 8 said he was also a man under authority. He submitted to the authority over him, therefore he had authority where he needed it. He acknowledged Jesus as also a man under authority. Jesus acknowledged this as faith. Knowing who is in authority and when you are in authority is important. Do not take authority when God would not want you to. The centurion knew when to submit under authority. When you are responsible to make a decision then God will also give you the authority and the grace to carry it out. We are responsible for the decisions we make. The first question to be asked should always be; "is this my decision to make?" When it is not your responsibility to make the decision, submit to the one that God has given the authority to. This will bring grace into your life. In Matthew 28, Jesus says, "all authority has been given to Me."

Matthew 28 tells us of the wonderful story of the women going to the tomb early in the morning, wondering who would roll away the stone. The stone was rolled away, the Lord had risen, and an angel met them. Rejoicing, they went to tell the disciples. On the way they meet Jesus. Later, He spoke to them, The Great Commission. Each one of us needs a plan on how we would teach a person who has come to Christ. If you have never thought of this before, do so now. In Hebrews 6:1-2, the basic teachings about Christ are laid out. Ask the Lord for a plan on how He would have you explain these things in a way, that the new believer would serve God the rest of his life. This is what kingdom living is all about. As we submit to His authority, go in His Name, we will have authority to go make disciples.

The Promise: authority as you go in His name, He is with us always.

The Condition: Going in the Name of Jesus; for He has conquered all things. He has risen. Making disciples, convincing people to live for Christ.

Take time to memorize the verse. Write it on a card, carry it with you, repeat it many times a day. Also memorize the reference. Read the entire chapter of Matthew 28, every day this week.
Let the word become flesh - a part of you!

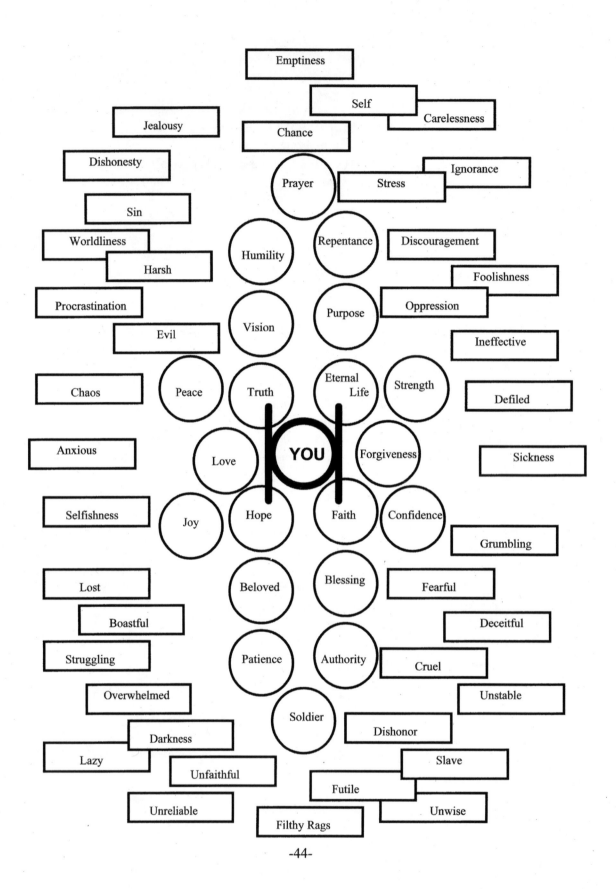

-44-

Soldier

Suffer hardship with me,
as a good soldier of Christ Jesus.
No soldier in active service
entangleth himself in the affairs
of every day life;
that he may please him
who enlisted him as a soldier.
II Timothy 2:3,4

How do we not get entangled in the affairs of every day life? God planted a garden, and put Adam into it to keep it, and care for it. There are many things in our place of living that God wants us to care for. He wants women to keep their houses so that peace and safety can be found there. He wants men to provide for their families. As we go about our work we need to keep our hearts in tune with the Father.

How do we do this? The answer is in Colossians3:23, "Whatever you do, do your work heartily, as for the Lord rather than for men." If you are doing something that you aren't doing for the Lord than stop doing it. Work is not a part of the curse. God wants us to work and He also wants us to rest. Ask Him how to arrange your work, what you should work and how you are to do it. "Commit thy works unto Jehovah, And your plans will be established," Proverbs 16:3. As you see that God wants you to work, it will make what you are doing purposeful and enjoyable. It was all God's plan.

God has a purpose in everything you are doing. Find that purpose and it will make work easier. We get entangled in our every day affairs when we separate work and spirituality. Sometimes we think, we will spend thus and thus time with God and then we are free to get on with our lives. God wants to be a part of everything we do. He is concerned about every little detail, and wants for you to share it with Him all day long. In this way we will not be entangled in the affairs of every day life. When we cleanse ourselves from these things, we are a vessel of honor, sanctified, useful to the Master, prepared for every good work, (v.21). These things (things we need to cleanse ourselves from) are found in verses 14 and 16.

The Promise: we will please the One who has enlisted us, Christ Jesus our Lord.

The Condition: doing everything heartily as to the Lord.

You now have four blessings carrying you, three on either side, five going ahead of you and five coming behind you. This looks pretty safe. Do you want to stop or will you continue to fortify yourself?

Take time to memorize the verse. Write it on a card, carry it with you, repeat it many times a day. Also memorize the reference. Read the entire chapter of II Timothy 2, every day this week.
Let the word become flesh - a part of you!

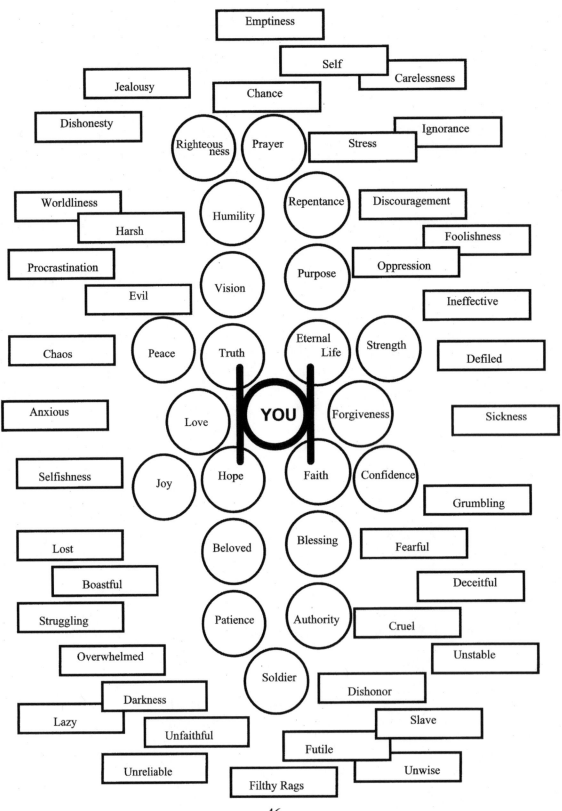

Righteousness

**for the kingdom of God is
not eating and drinking,
but
righteousness and peace
and joy in the Holy Ghost.
Romans 14:17**

Righteousness is the breastplate of the armor of God. It means, not guilty. Right and just can be interchanged. On the cross Jesus was made sin for our sinfulness that we might be made righteous with His righteousness. We were justified (just-as-if-I-had-never-sinned). Or we could say rightified. This then is the breastplate that covers our heart, bringing us to Romans 8:1, "There is therefore now no condemnation for those who are in Christ Jesus." We are free from the law of sin and death.

Matthew 6:33, "But seek first His kingdom and His righteousness and all these things shall be added to you." These things meaning food and drink. Romans 14:17 says, "the kingdom of God is righteousness, peace and joy." Peace we must pursue, (run after it) joy comes from being in fellowship with God. Peace and joy are both fruits of the Spirit. In the verse, notice, the kingdom of God is righteousness, peace and joy in the Holy Spirit. It is in the Holy Spirit, living by the Spirit, walking in the Spirit, that makes the difference.

Romans 10, tells us, they who did not know about God's righteousness tried to establish their own. Our own righteousness is as filthy rags, Isaiah 64:6. God's righteousness is first hearing the Word, secondly thinking on it, and letting it come into our hearts. Then it becomes faith and we believe. The result of this being, God's righteousness. Abraham believed, and faith was reckoned to Him as righteousness. This is God's righteousness.

Christ is our righteousness. By faith we move out of our ourselves - into Christ; out of our sin - into His righteousness; out of our weakness - into His power; out of our failure - into His victory; out of our limitations - into His omnipotence.

The Promise: serving Christ in this way, you are acceptable to God, and approved by men It is in Christ that we are righteous. Righteousness in the Holy Spirit, (being right) means not guilty.

The Condition: based on faith, which comes by hearing. So hearing the word, meditating on it, letting it become faith, believing what was heard. This then results in righteousness.

Take time to memorize the verse. Write it on a card, carry it with you, repeat it many times a day. Also memorize the reference. Read the entire chapter of Romans 14, every day this week.
Let the word become flesh - a part of you!

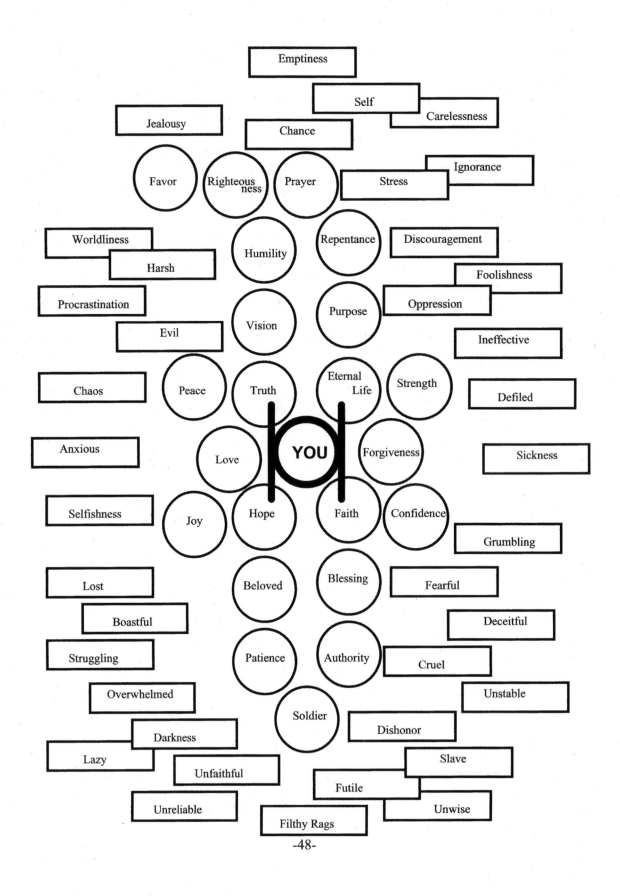

-48-

Favor

Do not let kindness and truth leave you,
Bind them around your neck,
Write them on the tablet of your heart.
So you will find favor and good repute
In the sight of God and man.
Proverbs 3:3,4

In Acts 7:10, Stephen is preaching. Starting with Abraham he expounded to them God's way with the children of Israel. In verse 10 he says Joseph found favor with the king of Egypt and he was made governor over all Egypt. This is food for thought. The story is long. At the least this story is twenty years long. There were times when Joseph did not feel favor in his life at all. What we can see though in Joseph's life in all that he did, there was displayed kindness and truth in it. Even though life was dealt disfavorably toward him at times, he was true to the commandments of God, and kind to the people around him. When you find yourself in a hard place, choose to respond with truth and kindness.

When we look at Joseph's life we can see the favor of God came because of his choice to live in truth and kindness in the hard times of his life. Even when he received favor and was next in line to the king of Egypt, facing his brothers was hard. Even though we receive favor, it does not mean that we will not have any difficult things come up in our lives.

Being kind consists of being friendly, generous, showing sympathy or being understanding. It's being sensitive to the other person's needs. Be a servant on purpose. How do we do that?, you might ask. Set out on your day's journey determined that you will be a servant, today. Then look for a need. As you do this day after day, you will become a kind person. Remember: Col.3:23, "Whatever you do, do your work heartily, as for the Lord rather than for men." When you do it for the Lord always, you will find that it's okay if it's your family that you are serving.

It is not always popular, nor is it easy to stand for truth. But at the end you will be rewarded for it by favor. When you live a life of repentance, and you find yourself in the wrong, you need to admit it. If you are right, be fit to live with. Don't move from the truth, but don't make a big fuss about how right you are either.

The Promise: Favor will come your way

The Condition: Bind kindness and truth around your neck. Write them on the tablet of your heart. Keep them close to your heart.

Take time to memorize the verse. Write it on a card, carry it with you, repeat it many times a day. Also memorize the reference. Read the entire chapter of Proverbs 3, every day this week.
Let the word become flesh - a part of you!

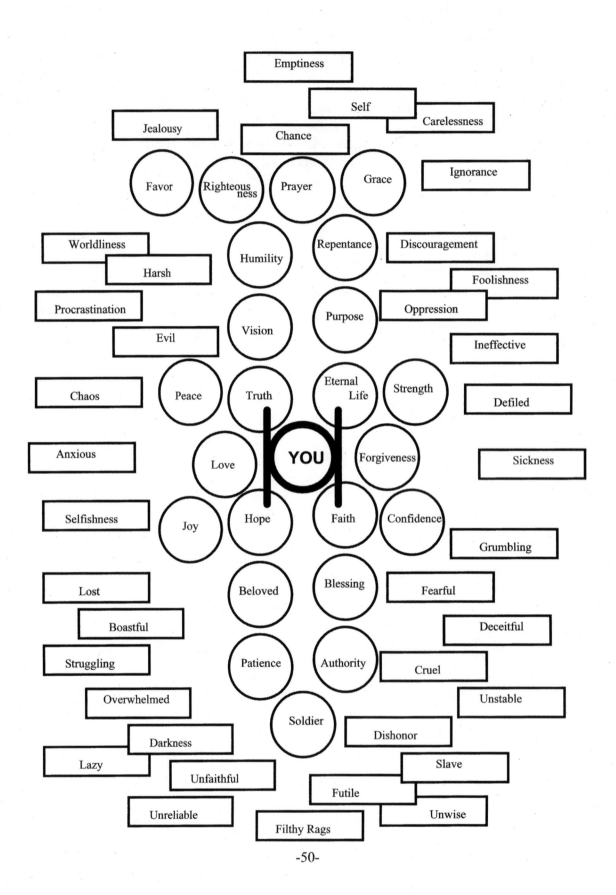

-50-

Grace

**for by grace
have ye been saved through faith;
and that not of yourselves,
it is the gift of God;
Ephesians 2:8**

God's grace is the reason you are saved. Grace is an ingredient that makes things work. It makes everything flow smoothly, like oil in an engine, or baking soda in a cake. God's grace toward us is a gift. He being rich in mercy and because of His great love, brought us both (Gentiles and Jews) who were far away from Him, near. The grace of God put it into action. Through the cross, (payment for sin) through the Blood that Jesus shed for us, we now have access in the Spirit to the Father. God's mercy plus God's love equals God's grace. Mercy + love = grace It is His grace that saved us.

As you come into a lifestyle of repentance, cultivate a humble attitude, and cast all your cares upon the Father all day long, this grace will then work in your life. Grace comes when you need it, and not ahead of time, for it is a gift of God. This is why when you look ahead to a difficult task, you do not seem to find the grace to carry it out. But when you get there, "His grace is sufficient."

When grace is at work in your life, you don't have to strive to try to make things work. They just work. When you have prayed about it more than you talked about it, than you have taken it to God. When your life seems to be too busy, take more time praying. Pray about everything on your agenda. Praying brings grace, this then brings peace. This cleanses us from the desires of the flesh, it cleanses us from the desires of the mind (v.3). Grace works in us when the flesh dies. Paul says, I die daily (I Cor.15:31), it's a daily battle.

God formed Adam from the dust of the earth. He then blew breath into this lifeless body, and he became a living soul. The body made of earth has a strong pull downward, and the breath (Spirit) being from heaven has a strong pull upward. Therefore our desires are of two sources. Dying to the desires of the flesh, comes about as we accept Christ's crucifixion in our stead, Galatians 2:20. Knowing that when Christ was crucified, "I was crucified with Him. It is no longer I that lives, but Christ lives in me, and the life that I now live in the flesh, I live by faith in the Son of God, who loved me, and delivered Himself up for me. I do not nullify the grace of God."

The Promise: grace in your life, that will help things to work smoothly.

The Condition: quit trying to do things on your own, having faith, (believe) in the grace of God

Take time to memorize the verse. Write it on a card, carry it with you, repeat it many times a day. Also memorize the reference. Read the entire chapter of Ephesians 2, every day this week.
Let the word become flesh - a part of you!

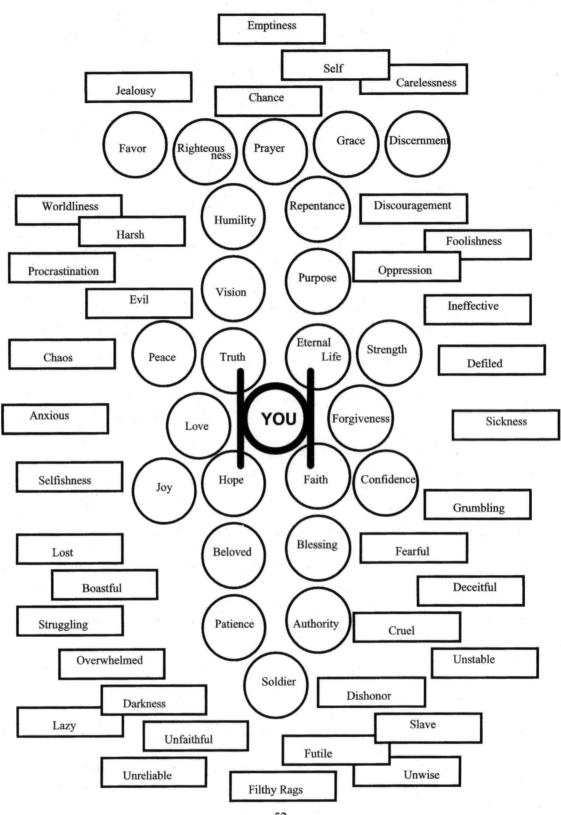

-52-

Discernment

Word of Wisdom, Word of Knowledge, Prophecy
Faith, Gifts of Healings, Working of Miracles
Discerning of Spirits, Various kinds of Tongues
Interpretation of Tongues
But one and the same Spirit works all these things
distributing to each one individually as He wills.
I Corinthians 12:8-11

These are the nine spiritual gifts of the Holy Spirit. They are manifestations of the Holy Spirit in your life. Discernment is being able to know if spirits are good or evil, light or darkness. "God has delivered us from the domain of darkness and transferred us to the kingdom of His beloved Son," Colossians 1:13. We are so used to ideas of the kingdom of darkness, that we have a hard time discerning the difference. The more you know God, the more you will understand His ways.

How do we discern the difference? In verse 3 of I Corinthians 12, he specifically tells us how to do that. "No one speaking by the Spirit of God says, "Jesus is accursed"; and no one can say, "Jesus is Lord" except by the Holy Spirit." This is a measuring stick with which we might discern the spirits. Studying Psalms 23 will also teach you what is from God and what is not. You will want to know God and become His friend, page 81. As you walk with God in your life, you will begin to understand the difference between good and evil. God is a God of peace. If it is not peaceful, then it is not from God. This is not difficult to discern, when we keep in mind, that there are just two sources, good and evil. Either it is God, or it isn't God, working in a situation.

The gifts of the Spirit are for the common good of all. This is why Paul continues on in telling us about how the body functions in chapter twelve. The gifts of the Spirit are beneficial only when used in love. This includes discernment. To use it in any other way is wrong, and is not the reason why God gave it to you. When God gives you discernment He will also give you direction whether or when to share it. Many times He only wants you to pray about.

You now have nine blessings going ahead of you, along with the four who are carrying you. There are three on either side, and five coming behind you. You are beginning to walk like a king.

The Promise: you will know what is right to do in every situation. (what would Jesus do?)

The Condition: to keep in mind, there are only two sources of all things on earth, the good and the evil. The good being from God and the evil is either from the devil, the flesh, or the world.

Take time to memorize the verse. Write it on a card, carry it with you, repeat it many times a day. Also memorize the reference. Read the entire chapter of I Corinthians 12, every day this week. **Let the word become flesh - a part of you!**

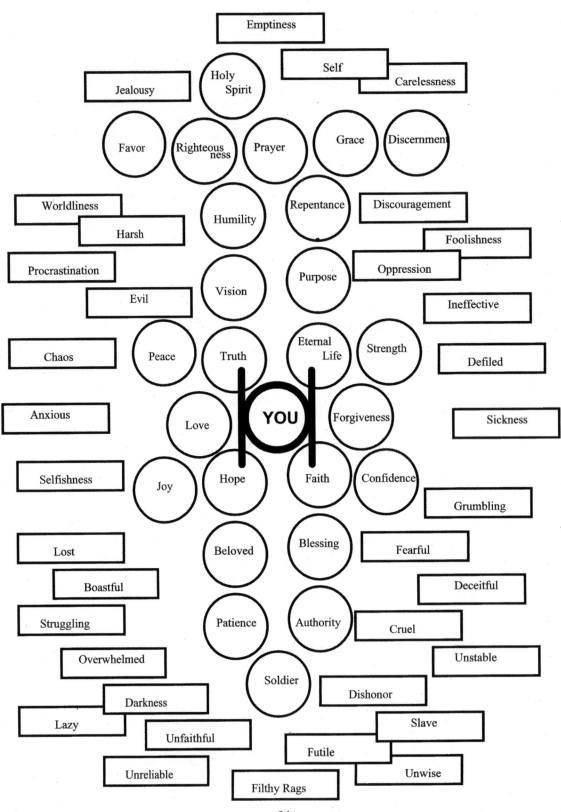

Holy Spirit

**And I will pray the Father,
and he shall give you another Helper,
that he may be with you for ever,
John 14:16**

God is a triune God. He is Father, Son, and Holy Spirit. The Spirit was moving over the earth before it was formed, Gen.1:2. It was the Spirit of God that drew you to know Jesus, to accept Him as your personal Savior, I Peter 1:2. Matthew tells us in 3:11, that John baptized "with water for repentance, but He (Jesus) will baptize you with the Holy Spirit and fire." Jesus Himself commanded His disciples, "Not to leave Jerusalem, but to wait for what the Father had promised," which, He said, "you heard of from Me; for John baptized with water, but you shall be baptized with the Holy Spirit..." Acts 1:4-5.

Mankind was separated from God the Father when sin became a part of their being. Jesus was born a man, lived on earth, died for sin and was buried. He overcame death and arose from the dead. This He did in our stead, our debt of sin was paid. When we accept Him, we have peace with God the Father. We can again communicate with Him. Jesus now ministers the Holy Spirit to us. He says He will send us a Helper, "Because He abides with you, and will be in you," (v.17). Later, (v.26) He says, "the Helper, the Holy Spirit, whom the Father will send in My Name, He will teach you all things, and bring to your remembrance all that I said to you." It is important that You receive the Holy Spirit into your life. That is God's avenue to speak to you. You do this by asking, Luke 11:13. He is a very gentle loving person, and He will be with you as a child of God. If you ask Him, He will come into you and bring the gifts along. "But you shall receive power when the Holy Spirit has come upon you, and you shall be My Witnesses......" Acts 1:8. To be a witness that will draw others to Christ, is only accomplished through the Holy Spirit. Romans 8 and Galatians 5 both share about living in the Spirit, (Ro.8:14; Gal.5:16). To be led by the Spirit, you need to hear what He is saying. The key is to be listening. Expect the Holy Spirit to talk to you. He is trustworthy. Trust Him!!

It is important that you are at peace, if you want to hear the Spirit. He will not speak when you are frustrated. There are times when we need to quiet ourselves, so that we are able to hear. He speaks gently, then you choose if you will obey or not. The more you obey, the more you get to know Him, the more you hear Him. He will never speak opposite to what the Word tells us. The Spirit and the Word always agree.

The Promise: you receive the Holy Spirit in your life when you ask. He is your Helper.

The Condition: to acknowledge the Holy Spirit as a Person and ask Him to rest upon you,

Take time to memorize the verse. Write it on a card, carry it with you, repeat it many times a day. Also memorize the reference. Read the entire chapter of John 14, every day this week.
Let the word become flesh - a part of you!

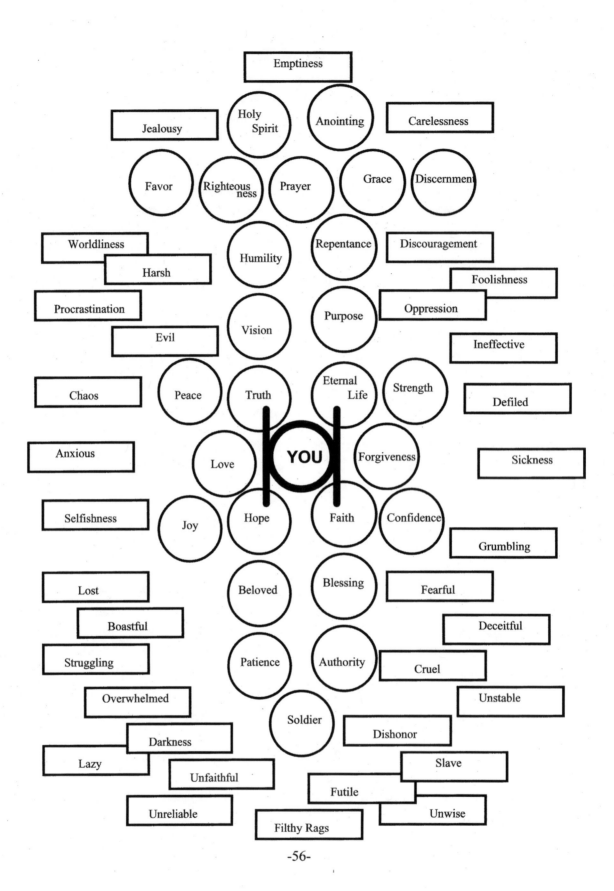

Anointing

**While we look not
at things which are seen,
but - at things which are not seen,
for the things - which are seen are temporal,
but the things - which are not seen are eternal.
II Corinthians 4:18**

This is a continuation of the Person of the Holy Spirit. And it could all be said, by quoting (v.7) in chapter 5 "for we walk by faith, not by sight." God dwelling in me, this is what the anointing is. God working through me and through you. This does not mean that you are not doing anything, but rather that you are doing much. But what you are doing, you are doing in the power of God (4:7). His hand is upon you.

Especially when you minister, whatever you are doing or saying in the anointing will touch the other person deeply. Whereas when done without the anointing, it seems to make little difference. Luke 4:18, Jesus speaking, "the Spirit of the Lord is upon Me, because He anointed Me to preach the gospel to the poor. He has sent Me to proclaim release to the captives, and recovery of sight to the blind, to set free those who were down trodden, to proclaim the favorable year of the Lord." It's all about the other person, not you. God's hand is upon you so that others might be touched.

The anointing comes on you when the flesh has been crucified, and you rest in God. Things that seemed very hard to do or comprehend are quite easy, when the anointing comes.

The one who anoints us is God, II Corinthians 1:21. (v.22) "who also sealed us and gave the Spirit in our hearts as a pledge." In times of old, the kings were called anointed ones, they were anointed by prophets acting on God's behalf. They ruled as God's representatives. The Priests also were anointed before they served, Ex.29:21. They served God and the people. Jesus has restored the authority of Adam to every believer. We are now anointed and appointed, kings and priests for each day we walk on earth.

The Promise: (4:6,7) God gives us light of the knowledge of the glory of God in the face of Christ. It is the surpassing greatness of the power of God (not from ourselves). We have this treasure in earthen vessels.

The Condition: looking to things you can not see with your eyes, you can not touch with your hands (many times the anointing can be felt). Remember: we walk by faith not by sight.

Take time to memorize the verse. Write it on a card, carry it with you, repeat it many times a day. Also memorize the reference. Read chapters 4 and 5 of II Corinthians, every day this week.
Let the word become flesh - a part of you!

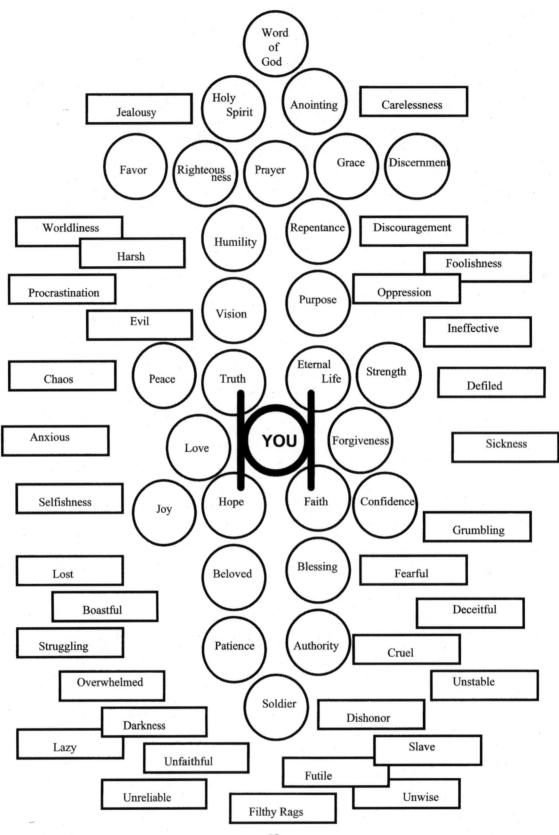

Word of God

**In the Beginning was the Word
and the Word was with God,
and the Word was God,
He was in the beginning with God.
John 1:1,2**

"He was in the beginning with God. All things came into being by Him, and apart from Him nothing came into being that has come into being." The Word of God is a Person, named Jesus. In Jesus was life (v.4) and light (v.5). Many people did not and still do not receive Him, but as many as do, have the right to become the children of God, (v.12). This is the will of God (v.13).

Going to Genesis 1, (v.1) in the beginning God created the heavens and the earth. (v.2) The Spirit of God was moving over the surface of the waters. (v.3) Then God said, and the Word of God created. What we see here is a triune God, Father, Son (the Word of God), Spirit (Holy Spirit) working together in unity. Each doing His part, in agreement with the other. Read John 1 and Genesis 1

In Luke 1:35, after Mary asked how shall this be, the angel answered, "The Holy Spirit will come upon you, and the power of the Most High will overshadow you." This Word became flesh, John 1:14. This is how the Word becomes flesh in you. It is when the Holy Spirit overshadows you, that the Word of God can do a work in you, and it becomes a part of you. This is how the Word became Man.

In Hebrews 4:12, "the Word of God is living and active and sharper than any two-edged sword, and piercing as far as the division of soul and spirit, of both joints and marrow (body) and the Word of God is able to judge the thoughts and the intentions of the heart." But then it reads (v.13), and there is no creature hidden from His sight, but all things are open and laid bare to the eyes of Him with whom we have to do." It is very clear that the Word of God is a Person.

The Word and the Spirit will always agree. Seeking the Spirit without the Word, or studying the Word apart from the Spirit, will make us go astray and miss God's plan.

The Condition:	**The Promise:**
When you:	It will:
read the Word -----------------------	cleanse you
meditate on the Word --------------------	strengthen you
study the Word -----------------------	build you

Take time to memorize the verse. Write it on a card, carry it with you, repeat it many times a day. Also memorize the reference. Read the entire chapter of John 1, every day this week.
Let the word become flesh - a part of you!

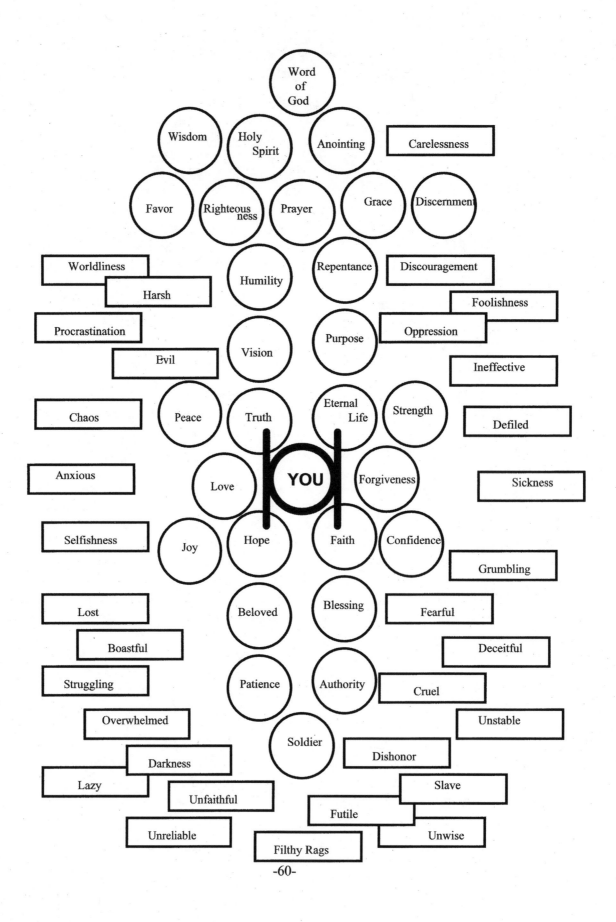

Wisdom

**But the Wisdom from above
is, first pure, then peaceful,
gentle, reasonable,
full of mercy, and good fruits,
unwavering, without hypocrisy
James 3:17**

In (v.13) James asks, "Who among you is wise and understanding?" As we read on we understand not all wisdom is from above. If we have wisdom from above let's show it by our good behavior in the gentleness of wisdom.

When there is jealousy and selfish ambition in your heart, the wisdom you have is earthly, natural, and demonic. We in our way of saying, would say of such a person, that he's a know-it-all. Even though you may be wise, and know many things, if your wisdom is not from above, it will only create a disorder and every evil thing.

The wisdom from above is first pure. It's a heart issue. To be pure, you must check your heart each day for things that need to be forgiven. It might be sin on your part that you need to ask God for forgiveness. Or there can be things you need to forgive others for, who have wronged you. Holding a grudge allows bitterness to creep in and your heart will no longer be pure. Also wisdom is peaceful. Peace we must seek after, pursue it, run after it. What are you willing to lay down for the sake of peace? Sometimes we have to fight for peace. In order to attain peace in any issue, you need to pray it through, before you approach it.

Gentleness connected to wisdom means tactful, speaking in such a way that people can receive what you are saying. Allowing God to show you the right timing. As we put away pride, we become more reasonable. It is being able to understand the other person's opinions. Full of mercy goes right along with that. Remember, the mercy God granted you.

Fruit is always the result of things that happened before. This is why good fruit is towards the end of this list. The sequence here is important. Unwavering, and without hypocrisy is simply a person that will not be moved, and is real to the core.

The Promise: you will become a wise person, a person with wisdom from above.

The Condition: asking God for wisdom, James 1:5. Keeping your heart and your motives right

Take time to memorize the verse. Write it on a card, carry it with you, repeat it many times a day. Also memorize the reference. Read the entire chapter of James 3, every day this week.
Let the word become flesh - a part of you!

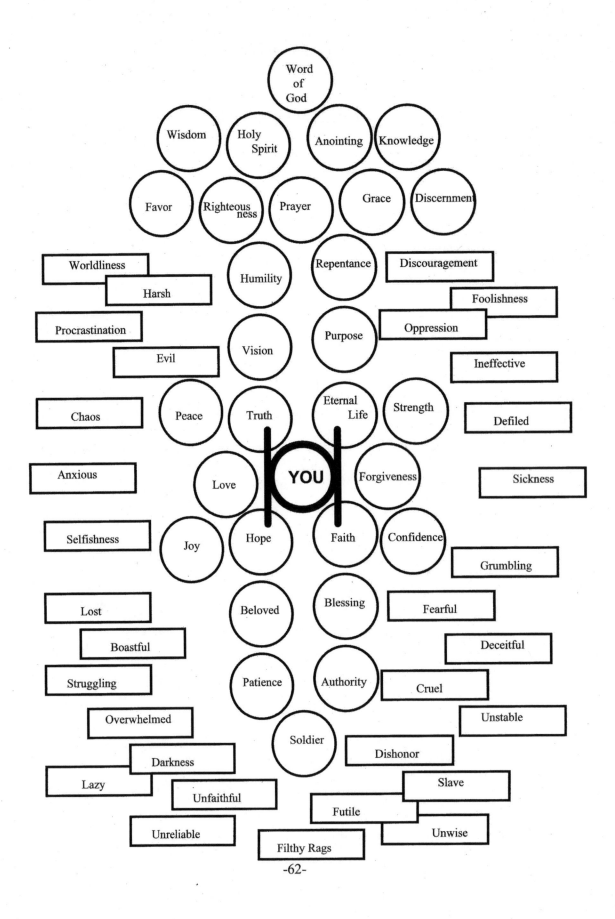

-62-

Knowledge

And this I pray,
that your love may abound
still more and more
in real knowledge and all discernment,
so that you may approve the things that are excellent.
Philippians 1:9-10a

What is real knowledge? Real knowledge comes as your love grows in God. In Ephesians One, Paul is praying for a revelation in the knowledge of God.

What do you know about God? When we know God our discernment increases. Knowledge of God comes by; studying the Word, seeking His face, and spending time with Him. This is a relationship, a relationship with God. The only way we have to get to know anyone is to spend time with them. Only when you have built a trust and confidence in someone will they share their deepest feelings with you. God is like that too. He will share Himself with those who spend time with Him.

Proverbs 1:7, "the fear of the Lord, is the beginning of knowledge." This means to respect Him for who He is. Who is God? What is He like? Psalms 103, talks a lot about God. (v.8), "He is compassionate and gracious, slow to anger and abounding in lovingkindness. But He will not always strive with us, nor will He keep His anger forever. At the same time He does not deal with us according to our sins, or iniquities. His lovingkindness is as high as the heavens. The Lord God has compassion on those who fear Him, He is very loving to us." On and on David goes explaining God.

To refresh yourself in the knowledge of God, reread the studies on Love and Blessings and find the one on the Fear of the Lord, page 101. Keep in mind that the whole Bible is meant to draw us into a relationship with God. Knowing God is real knowledge. Your love and knowledge of God is only as great as your love and knowledge of the Bible is. This is why mankind was created. So that God might have fellowship with us.

The Promise: you will approve things that are excellent, be sincere and blameless, (v.11) filled with fruit of righteousness

The Condition: Building a relationship with God

You now have 4 blessings carrying you, 3 on each side, 5 following you and 14 going before you

.
Take time to memorize the verse. Write it on a card, carry it with you, repeat it many times a day. Also memorize the reference. Read the entire chapter of Philippians 1, every day this week.
Let the word become flesh - a part of you!

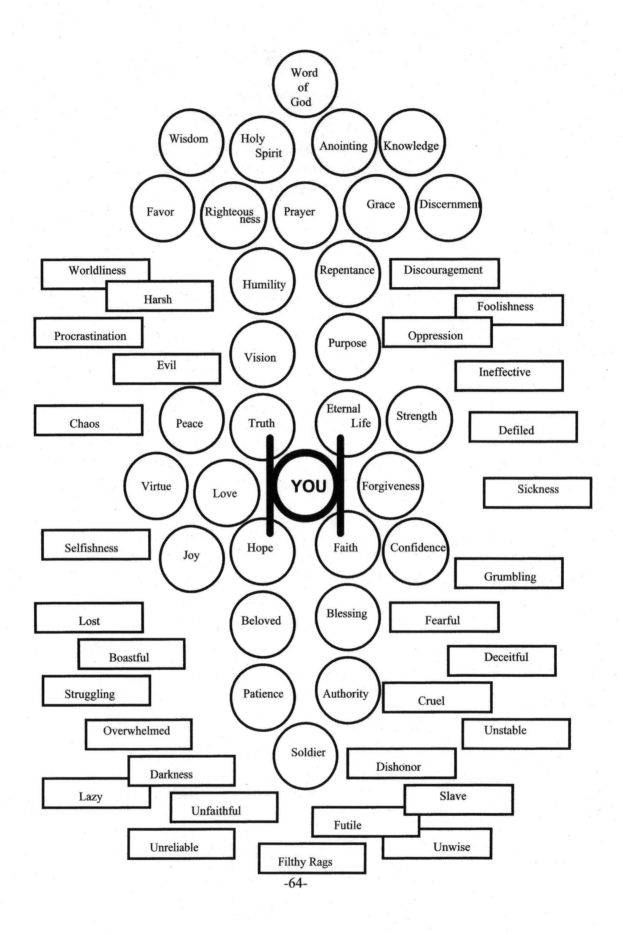

Virtue

Finally, brethren, whatever is true,
whatever is honorable, whatever is right,
whatever is pure, whatever is lovely,
whatever is of good repute,
if there be any excellence,
and if anything worthy of praise,
let your mind dwell on those things.
Philippians 4:8

I choose this verse to express virtue, because virtue comes from the heart. And the condition of our heart comes from what the mind meditates on. Proverbs 23:7, "for as he thinks within himself, so he is." You are what you think. Matthew 12:37, "for by your words you shall be justified, and by your words you shall be condemned." You speak what you think. You have a choice what you meditate on. When an evil thought comes into your mind, you have the choice if you will think about it or not.

Carefully read Philippians 4 and you will see how you can become virtuous. (v.4) rejoice always, (v.5) be kind and gentle to all people, (v.6) be anxious about nothing, but in everything let your requests be known to God in prayer with thanksgiving, (v.7) let the peace of God guard your hearts and minds. Then he says, "think on the right things." Again it's your choice what you think. God never asks us to do anything that we can't do. (v.12) Paul, knew how to get along with little, he knew how to get along with abundance. This is being content.

With this in place he says, "I can do all things through Him who strengthens me." This is a virtuous person. We read about the Proverbs 31 woman, she is a virtuous woman. I believe she said, "I can do all things through Christ who strengthens me." Then there is the blessed man in Psalms One, who meditates on the Word day and night. I Chronicles 4:10, Jabez called on the Lord that He would bless him and enlarge his territory. He asked that the Lord's hand would be upon him, that He would keep him from harm, and that he might not cause pain. These are virtuous people.

The Promise: God will supply all your needs, according to His riches in glory, in Christ - a virtuous person

The Condition: 1) rejoice always; 2) be gentle to all men; 3) let God's peace guard your heart and mind; 4) think on the right things; 5) live with what you have, much or not much.

Take time to memorize the verse. Write it on a card, carry it with you, repeat it many times a day. Also memorize the reference. Read the entire chapter of Philippians 4, every day this week.
Let the word become flesh - a part of you!

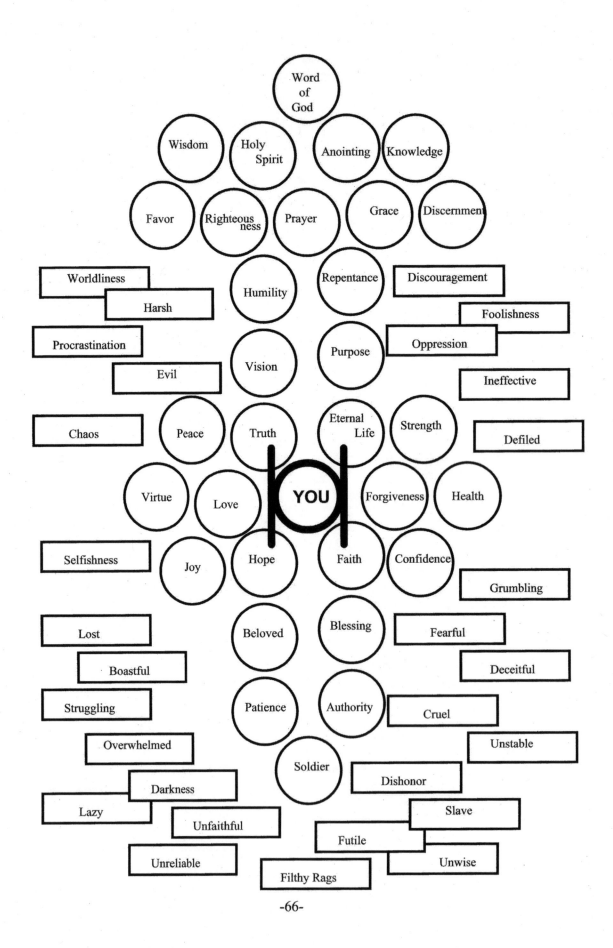

Health

My son, attend to my words;
Incline thine ear unto my sayings.
Let them not depart from your sight
Keep them in the midst of thy heart.
For they are life unto those that find them,
And health to all their whole body.
Proverbs 4:20-22

King Solomon wrote Proverbs, and the underlying theme to all of it, is wisdom. He did not write it in story form, but allowed himself to change the subject whenever he wanted to. There are many valuable nuggets in the book of Proverbs besides wisdom. These couple verses on health are one of those nuggets. You will greatly benefit from picking up this nugget and making a part of your life.

He talks about the mind, the ear, the eyes and the heart. It is with your minds that you listen. You listen to the things that you are most interested in. Incline your ear, or giving ear, it means you are teachable to what you are hearing. When you hear and believe, you act upon what you are hearing by faith. These verses are telling you that, it is the Word that you need to listen to, be teachable in, and focus your vision on. Then keep it in your heart, for your heart controls your life.

When you go to the Doctor, he will give you pills or medicine. Many times you are to take them four times a day, after each meal and at bedtime. To read the Word in this way, after meals and before bedtime will benefit you greatly, when sick.

He is talking of health here. It is good to exercise your body in order to stay healthy. The exercise of reading the Word will go a long way in keeping you healthy. Read it out loud. Look for a promise in the Word you are reading. Ask yourself how can I act upon it, to let it become a part of my life? Matthew 7:24, when you hear the Word of God, and act upon it, you will become a wise person. You also will become a healthy person.

The Promise: if you receive God's Word regularly through both the ear and the eye, so that it will occupy and control your heart, then you will find both life to our souls and health to your whole body.

The Condition: is four-fold: 1) give attention to My words (listen); 2) incline your ear (be teachable); 3) do not let them depart from your eyes (focused eyes) act upon what you hear in faith; 4) keep them in the midst of your heart, your heart controls your life.

Take time to memorize the verse. Write it on a card, carry it with you, repeat it many times a day. Also memorize the reference. Read the entire chapter of Proverbs 4, every day this week.
Let the word become flesh - a part of you!

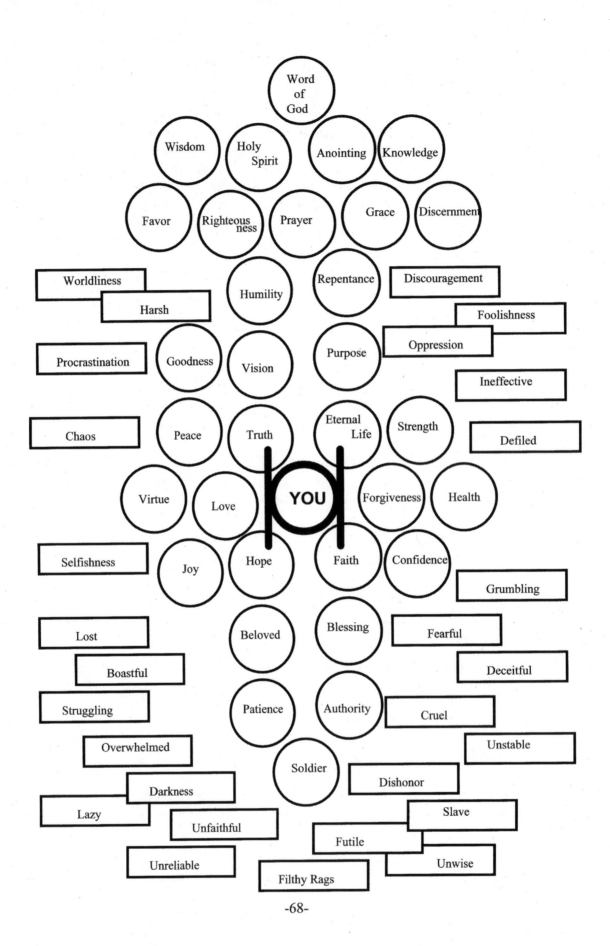

Goodness

Do not be overcome by evil,
but overcome evil with good.
Romans 12:21

Chapter 12 of Romans is a chapter that is loaded with life changing concepts. It is all summarized in this last verse. Many times we focus on the last part first. He first says, "do not be overcome with evil" (v.9), "abhor what is evil, hate it." You will not overcome what is a friend to you. In verse 1 it states, "present your bodies a living and holy sacrifice." God wants not only your heart, but your whole body and everything you do. Nothing less is acceptable, rather it is evil.

Micah says it well in (6:8), "He has told you, O man, what is good, And what does the Lord require of you? But to do justice, to love kindness, and to walk humbly before your God."

Romans 12:2, we can actually prove what is good, acceptable and perfect by renewing our minds. As we take verse one and two together. We can see that we need to do what our minds have realized. As the mind is transformed, so our way of responding to life must also change. This is a sacrifice of our body. Our bodies do not want to change. In verse 3 it says, "Do not think more highly of yourself than you ought to," remember you do not have all the answers, be teachable. You do have a measure of faith though that is uniquely yours. Try to understand where you fit in the body of Christ (v.4-8). What gift has God given you? Where does He want you to function? Don't try to be someone else. God wants all the body to function. What is most important to you, is not the most important to everyone else. It is though, an important part of many others.

Verse 9, be sincere, be real, don't pretend. The rest of the verse tells us how to do that. "Hate what is evil, and cling to what is good." As we read the Word, we must allow our belief system to be checked. (v.10) talks about humility; (v.11) doing everything heartily as unto the Lord, Col. 3:23. (v.12), not quitting; (v.13) sharing; (v.14) this speaks of our words and thoughts, they either bless or curse. I pray that my thoughts would bless those around me. Listen to what you are thinking. Is it blessing those around you? (v.15) be sensitive to those around you; (v.16) be agreeable; (v.17) live blameless; (v. 18) be at peace with all men (as much as possible) meaning you can not be at peace with their sins. (19) you don't need to settle it! God will. (v.20) live a life that will convict others.

The Promise: In this way you will not be overcome by evil, but overcome evil by good

The Condition: giving your body a living and holy sacrifice

Take time to memorize the verse. Write it on a card, carry it with you, repeat it many times a day. Also memorize the reference. Read the entire chapter of Romans 12, every day this week.
Let the word become flesh - a part of you!

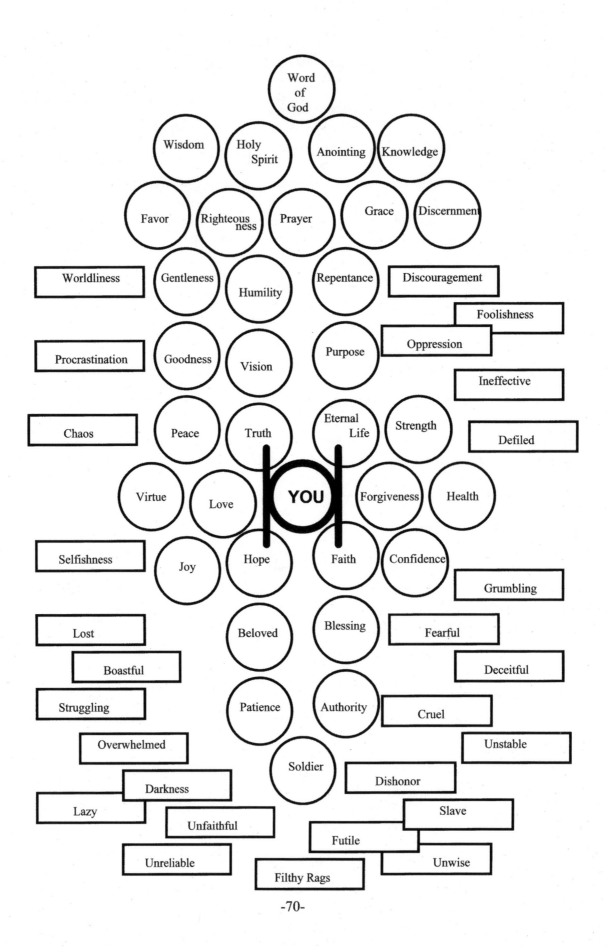

Gentleness

And let us not lose heart in doing good.
for in due time we shall reap
if we do not grow weary.
Galatians 6:9

Being gentle means being considerate. Verse 1 speaks of a spirit of gentleness. It is an attitude explained in (v.3) very well. We are a part of the body of Christ. We need the other parts as well. When we keep this in mind, we will become more gentle.

Gentleness is a fruit of the Spirit, chapter five. (v.25) "if we live by the Spirit, let us also walk by the Spirit." How to do this is what chapter six is all about.

When a person is caught in a trespass, we need to remember that we are not perfect either. In our eyes some sins are bigger than others. The key to this is in II Timothy 2:24-26. Don't get into an arguement with a person in sin, but with gentleness correct them. Keeping the goal in mind, that perhaps God would grant them repentance, leading them to the knowledge of truth and he would escape the snare of the devil. Only God can give freedom to another person, we can not. We need to work with God. Don't run ahead of God. Our attitude makes a great difference in the outcome, of such a situation. Are you there to help and restore a person caught in sin, or are you there to show them that you are more spiritual than he (she) is?

To genuinely have a love for a person, and see the good in them is so important. Every person has good in them. At times the good is buried under a ton of evil, where it is hard for you to see it. Remember, that person is less aware of the good in themselves, then you are.

Verse 7 is also a verse to meditate on and memorize. It will keep you from being deceived. The sowing and reaping process is a law of God that is at work in a vast part of our lives. The amount of effort you put in anything is what you will get out of it. How much time you spend also makes a difference. This is true in prayer, in eating, in relationships, and in many other areas as well. Decide what your priorities are and then spend your time and effort there.

The Promise: in due time you will reap

The Condition: (v.9) keeping on, keeping on doing good -- don't quit

Take time to memorize the verse. Write it on a card, carry it with you, repeat it many times a day. Also memorize the reference. Read the entire chapter of Galatians 6, every day this week.
Let the word become flesh - a part of you!

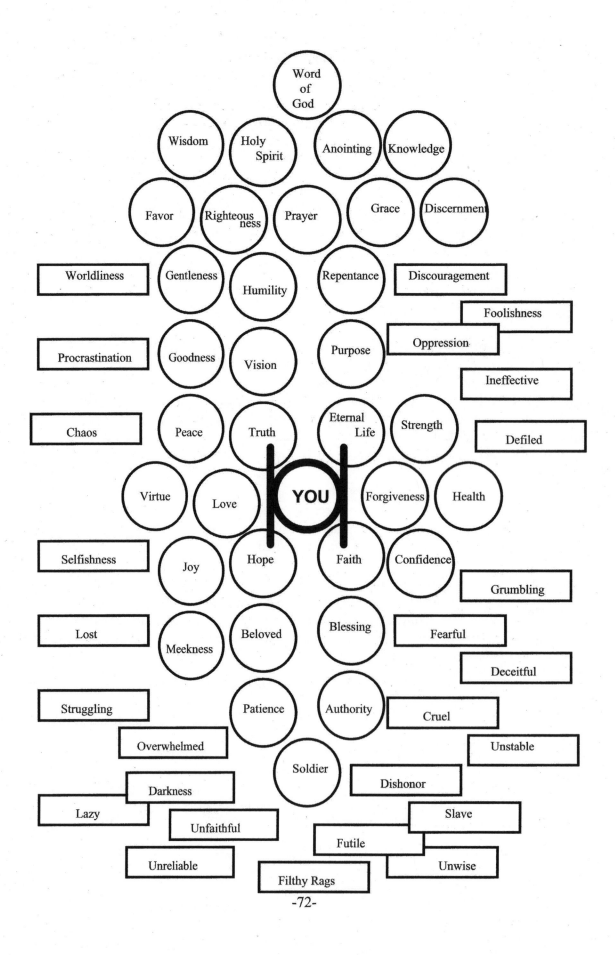

Meekness

I have been crucified with Christ,
and it is no longer I who live, but Christ lives in me;
and the life which I now live in the flesh
I live by faith in the Son of God,
who loved me, and delivered Himself up for me.
Galatians 2:20

In John 19, we read of Jesus being crucified. God in heaven gave Himself to die to sin, Romans 6:6. The body of sin was done away with, for he who has died is freed from sin. Romans 6:8, "if we have died with Christ, we will also live with Him." (v.10) "the death He died, He died to sin, once for all; but the life that He lives, He lives to God." The law tried to get everyone to do the right thing, and it just would not work, Galatians 3. Also in Hebrews 7, we read of a putting away of the law, of the old priesthood. "He (Jesus) is able to save forever those who draw near to God through Him, since He always lives to make intercession for them, (v.25)."

In John 20, we read of Jesus' resurrection. Even though they sealed the tomb, the stone was rolled away. Matthew 28:1-8 explains it more clearly. There was a severe earth quake, the stone was rolled away. An angel of the Lord sat on it. The guards shook for fear of Him (the angel) and became like dead men. The angel then spoke to the women saying that Jesus, who was crucified, is not here. He is risen! He told them to go and tell His disciples.

Jesus could have risen without the stone being removed. And think about this, why did the guards become as dead men, and the women didn't? The disciples and others saw Jesus before He went to heaven, many in Jerusalem did not. Think on these things.

Meekness is esteeming the other person higher than yourself, even when he's wrong. Know who you are, and whose you are. Numbers 12:3, Moses was the meekest (most humble) man on earth. Moses was fierce when sin had to be dealt with. Being meek does not mean you put up with just everything. It means you stand up for what is right, knowing Christ died for all sin, that all mankind might be set free. I Corinthians 1:29-31, a meek person is one who does not boast before God. It is because of what He (Jesus) did that we are in Christ Jesus. Jesus became to us wisdom from God and righteousness and sanctification and redemption. We must only boast in the Lord.

The Promise: the power and wisdom of God to flow through you, I Corinthians 1:24.

The Condition: reckoning yourself dead to sin, alive to God in Christ Jesus, Romans 6:11.

Take time to memorize the verse. Write it on a card, carry it with you, repeat it many times a day. Also memorize the reference. Read the entire chapter of Galatians 3, every day this week.
Let the word become flesh - a part of you!

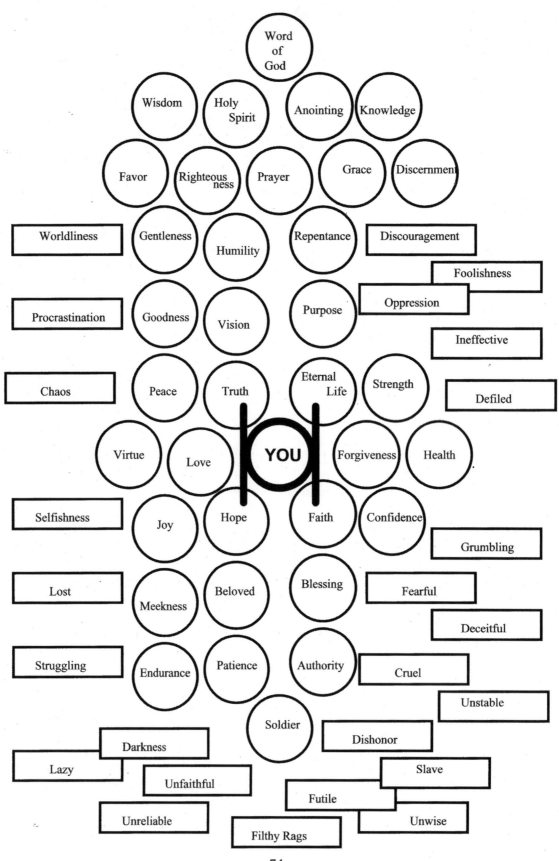

Endurance

**Count it all joy, my brethren,
when ye fall into manifold temptations;
Knowing that the proving of your faith
worketh patience.
And let patience have its perfect work,
that ye may be perfect and entire,
lacking in nothing.
James 1:2,3,4**

Who wants to think of trials as joy. Joy comes from knowing that you can talk to the Father about whatever your needs are and He will move on your behalf, John 16:24. You must keep in mind, when a trial comes, that God wants to work on your behalf. He wants you to ask Him what is on His heart. Then set your mind on the greatness of God, not on how bad the trial is.

I Corinthians 10:13, "No temptation has overtaken you but such as is common to man; and God is faithful, who will not allow you to be tempted beyond what you are able, but with the temptation will provide the way of escape also, that you may be able to endure it." Take time to also memorize this verse, especially the reference, so that you can turn to it in time of need. After you have earnestly prayed it a couple times you will remember it.

Pray something like this: Father in heaven, I know You are faithful and that You will not allow anything to come my way, but that You will also make a way through it. Show me the way through and then help me to walk through it.

It doesn't say He will show you the way around it, or that he will have it fade away, but that He will walk you through it. Remember: Hebrews 13:5, "I will never desert you, not will I forsake you." As you walk through a trial, God will do a work within you. Ask Him what He would want you to learn in this trial, that you could come out of it a better person. Notice, (v.12) of James 1, "blessed is a man who perseveres under trial; for once he has been approved, he will receive the crown of life, which the Lord has promised to those who love Him." Endurance and patience are not gifts of God, but rather fruits. Fruit is always the result of growth. Life will bring trials. Those trials can bear fruit or they can ruin you. The difference comes from how you respond.

The Promise: being a better person at the end of the trial

The Condition: going to the Lord for help in a time of trial

Take time to memorize the verse. Write it on a card, carry it with you, repeat it many times a day. Also memorize the reference. Read the entire chapter of James 1, every day this week.
Let the word become flesh - a part of you!

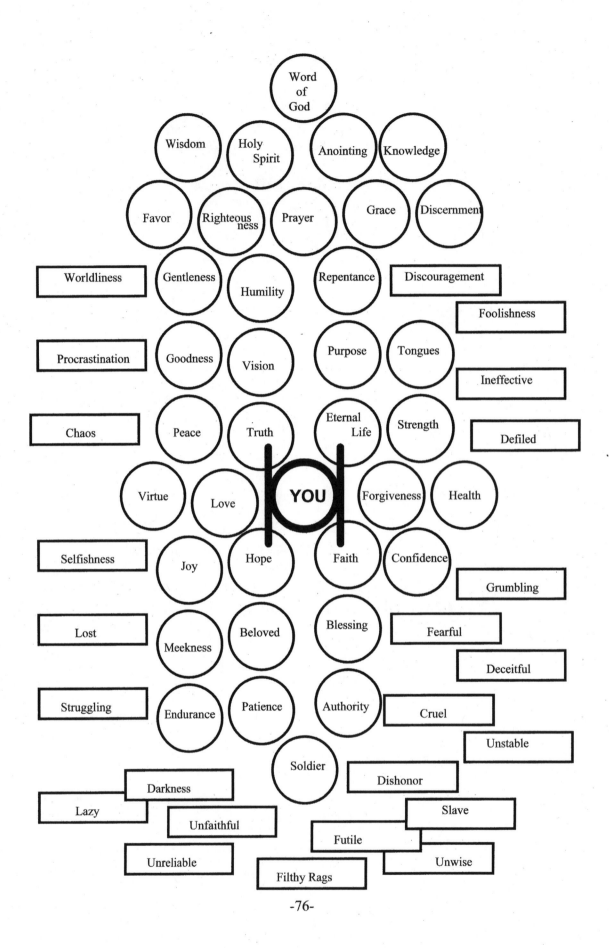

Tongues

He that speaketh in a tongue edifies himself;
but he that prophesies edifies the church.
I Corinthians 14:4

For forty days, Jesus was on earth after His resurrection. He appeared to His disciples in those days and spoke to them things concerning the kingdom of God. When He was ready to ascend to the Father (Acts 1:4,5), "He commanded them not to leave Jerusalem, but to wait for what the Father had promised." "Which, He said, You have heard of from Me; for John baptized with water, but you shall be baptized with the Holy Spirit not many days from now."

Acts 1:8, "but you shall receive power when the Holy Spirit has come upon you; and you shall be My witnesses." You would do well to read all of Acts 1 and 2. The disciples waited in an upper room praying and fasting for ten days. Then Jesus baptized them in the Holy Spirit, they were filled with the Spirit and spoke with other tongues. These men were so ready to have the power that Jesus was telling them about, that they waited ten days for Him to come. They believed what He was saying was true.

The Holy Spirit does more than give you an utterance in tongues. Tongues are given by the Holy Spirit to edify yourself, Eph.6:18. First you need to understand who you are. I Thessalonians 5:23, we read, "now the God of peace Himself sanctify you entirely, may your spirit and soul and body be preserved completely ...." This helped me to understand better the fact that, I am a spirit, I live in a body, and I have a soul. The soul is your mind, will and emotions. Let me verify this very briefly. Ephesians 2:1, "you were dead in your trespasses and sins." "You were dead" was not your body, nor was it your soul (mind, will, or emotions), it was your spirit. II Cor.5:1-4, Paul talks to us about living in this tent, meaning the body. Romans 12 is a good chapter to read concerning the soul. It talks about renewing the mind, about aligning our will with God's will and about many attitude issues.

The Holy Spirit came to the disciples to give them power to witness. The purpose of tongues has not changed. Tongues strengthens you in the spirit. It is your spirit that the Holy Spirit communicates with. So then, speaking in tongues will enlarge your spirit man and the other gifts of the Spirit will work more freely through you. Always remember that the gifts flowing through you are for the purpose of drawing others to God, and as you do that God will encourage you. How do we receive tongues? The answer is in Luke 11:13, "the Father will give the Holy Spirit to those who ask Him."

The Promise: power to witness

The Condition: ask and you shall receive

Take time to memorize the verse. Write it on a card, carry it with you, repeat it many times a day. Also memorize the reference. Read the entire chapter of I Corinthians 14, every day this week.
Let the word become flesh - a part of you!

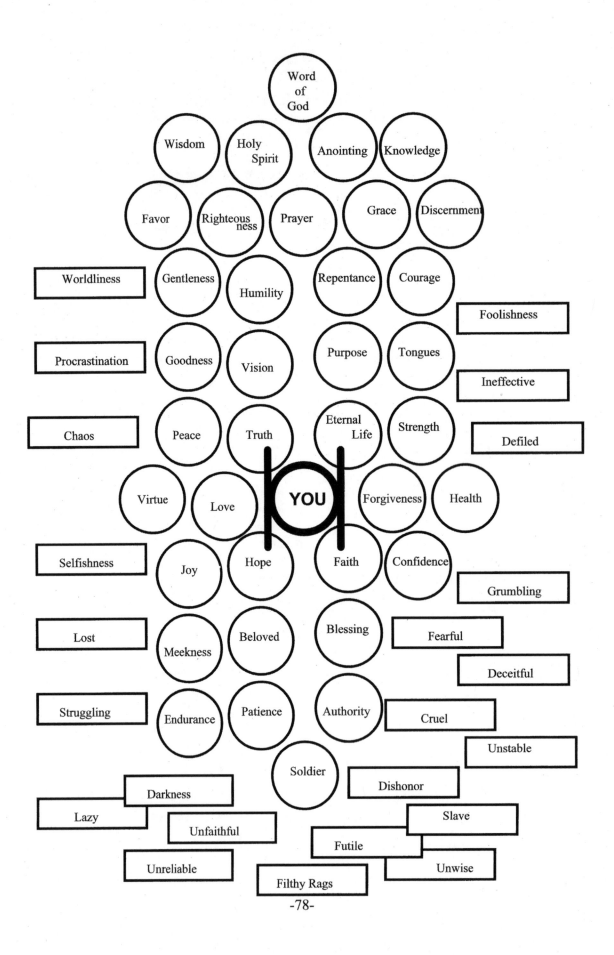

Courage

**The thief cometh not, but that he may
steal, and kill, and destroy:
I came that they may have life,
and may have it abundantly.
John 10:10**

When we have life, we have courage. When Moses died, the Lord commanded Joshua to "be strong and courageous, do not tremble or be dismayed, for the Lord your God is with you wherever you go." Joshua followed that command and at the end He could say, (24:15) "as for me and my house, we have chosen to serve the Lord."

The whole gospel of John speaks about the fact that Jesus is life. In John 10:11, Jesus tells us He is the good Shepherd. A good Shepherd will lay down his life for the sheep. This He has done (v.18). The Shepherd of our soul has laid down His life, so that we might have life and have it more abundantly. Abundance speaks of life in totality, spiritually and physically. Everything in every way is either life or death. Bring Jesus into every area of your life. Talk to Him about your cares, I Peter 5:7. There is nothing too big or too small to take to Him. Living is the opposite of death. Resting, eating, and sleeping are the main functions of your body. When you are at rest, eating right, and getting enough sleep, there is more life within you. You have more to offer as a sacrifice.

Live in Psalms 23, and you will be able to obey the command spoken to Joshua for us, "be strong and courageous." There is much courage in this passage. You can discern what is from God and what is not from God by studying it. God will not just be there for you, but He will lead you. He will restore you and give you rest when you need it. Listen to what He is saying and follow Him. The result is: abundance.

"The Lord is my Shepherd, I shall not want. He maketh me to lie down in green pastures; He leadeth me beside still waters. He restoreth my soul: He leads me in the paths of righteousness for His name's sake. Yea, though I walk through the valley of the shadow of death, I will fear no evil; for thou art with me; Thy rod and thy staff, they comfort me. Thou preparest a table before me in the presence of mine enemies: Thou hast anointed my head with oil; My cup runneth over. Surely goodness and lovingkindness shall follow me all the days of my life; And I shall dwell in the house of the Lord forever.

The Promise: - life and life more abundantly

The Condition: - following the source of life, Jesus the good Shepherd.

Take time to memorize the verse. Write it on a card, carry it with you, repeat it many times a day. Also memorize the reference. Read the entire chapter of John 10, every day this week.
Let the word become flesh - a part of you!

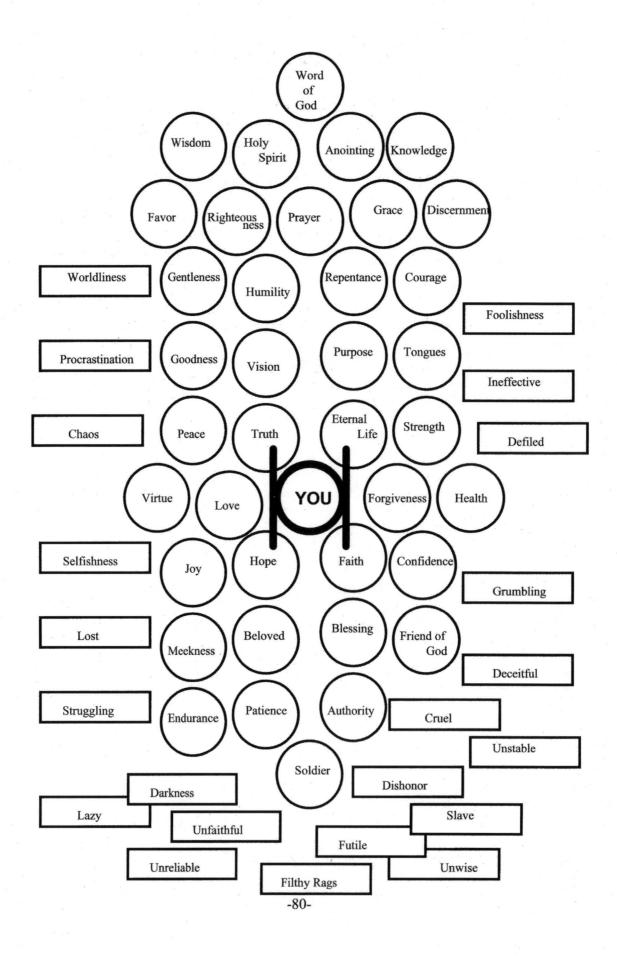

Friend of God

No longer do I call you servants;
for the servant knoweth not
what his Lord doeth:
but I have called you friends;
for all things that I heard from my Father,
I have made known unto you.
John 15:15

In James 2:23, Abraham was called "the friend of God." Genesis 18:17, the Lord said, "Shall I hide from Abraham what I am about to do?" He goes on to say that Abraham will surely become a great and mighty nation, in him all the nations of the earth will be blessed, for He had chosen him. And God told Abraham all that He was about to do. Abraham then interceded for every righteous person in Sodom and Gomorrah (this saved Lot's life). They shared their heart's concerns. Friends are those you can confide in, being able to tell them what's really on your heart.

Many times we read that God spoke to Abraham. Abraham's life starts in Genesis 11 and ended in chapter 25, thirteen chapters later. There are many lessons we can take from the life of Abraham, who was at first Abram until God changed His name. What God says in the New Testament about a person of the Old Testament has great significance. In Romans 5, we read about his faith (believing) in God being counted to him for righteousness. Galatians 3, again tells us that his righteous was by faith, and adds that the promises of Abraham were to him and his seed. That seed being Jesus. Hebrews 7, shares about the king of Salem, Melchizedek, blessing Abraham. Again and again we read of Abraham throughout the Word of God. James wrapped it up, saying he was "the friend of God." God and Abraham shared their hearts together. There was nothing they didn't share with one another.

Jesus has called us friends. This is a calling from God. He wants to share His deepest concern with us. He wants to hear our deepest concerns. Jesus is saying, that God will be glorified, when you bear much fruit. In this way you will prove that you are His disciple (v.8). He chose you and appointed you to bear fruit, fruit that remains. In the middle of this He talks of calling you, His friend. This is the key to the chapter of John 15, to be a friend of God. Get connected to Him, and stay connected. Studying the life of Abraham will help you to understand what it means to be a friend of God. Then you will bear fruit.

The Promise: much fruit

The Condition: taking time to become God's friend

Take time to memorize the verse. Write it on a card, carry it with you, repeat it many times a day. Also memorize the reference. Read the entire chapter of John 15, every day this week.
Let the word become flesh - a part of you!

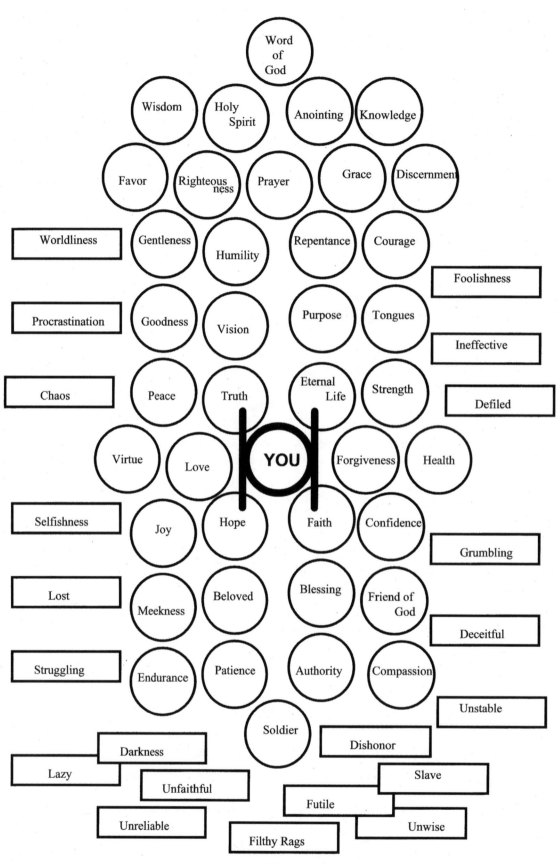

Compassion

Be ye kind one to another,
tenderhearted, forgiving each other,
even as God also in Christ forgave you.
Ephesians 4:32

Compassion is an issue of the mind which flows out of your heart. This can become a part of your life only when you become renewed in the spirit of your mind, and lay aside the old self.

Ephesians 4:17 through 31, talks about many practical issues that need to be dealt with in your life. These are issues that we all have to confront before any one of us can accomplish verse 32.
1) the futility of the mind; (v.17) the things that your mind is focused on that is of no purpose
2) the hardness of your heart; (v.18) sin will harden your heart
3) being greedy; (v.19) things that benefit me
4) lusts of deceit, falsehood; (v.22) a desire to do things that are not according to the truth
5) stealing; (v.28) wanting and taking what you did not work for
6) unwholesome words; (v.29) words that do not edify the hearer
7) bitterness; (v.31) the result of unforgiveness
8) wrath; (v,31) active anger
9) anger; (v.31) a feeling of extreme displeasure toward someone or something
10) clamor; (v.31) an expression (loud outcry) of protest
11) slander; (v.31) the putting down of another's reputation
12) malice; (v.31) a desire to harm others or to see them suffer "You did not learn Christ in this way
If indeed you have heard Him and have been taught in Him" (v.20-21)

Truth is in Jesus
1) renewed in the mind; (v.23) live a repentant life
2) Put on the new self; (v.24) "which is in likeness of God, created in righteousness and holiness"
3) speak truth; (v.25)- about your neighbor - everyone in your life
4) do not give the devil an opportunity; (v.27) do not sin knowingly
5) work with your hands; (v.28) work is not a part of the curse
6) speak words that bring edification and grace to the hearer; (v.29) think before you speak
7) do not grieve the Holy Spirit; (v.30) obey His promptings

The Promise: becoming compassionate

The Condition: confronting the issues in your life that are not right, then yielding to the Spirit of God to replace them with His ways.

Take time to memorize the verse. Write it on a card, carry it with you, repeat it many times a day. Also memorize the reference. Read Ephesians 4:17-32, every day this week.
Let the word become flesh - a part of you!

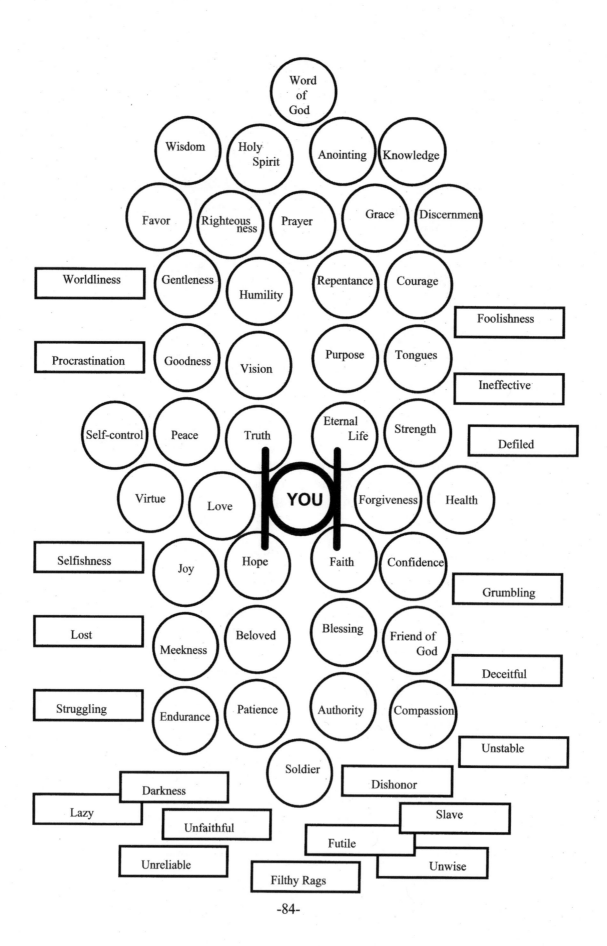

Self-Control

**For if these qualities are yours
and are increasing
they render you neither useless nor unfruitful
in the true knowledge
of our Lord Jesus Christ
II Peter 1:8**

What qualities is he talking about here that need to be increasing in our lives? That answer is found in: verse 5,6,7: faith, virtue (moral excellent), knowledge, self-control, perseverance, godliness, brotherly love, and unconditional love. These are the steps through every obstacle in your life.

No one on this earth will ever come to the point where these qualities should not continue to increase. But self-control is very much the most important link here. God gives us faith so that we can live a good moral life and gain the knowledge of God, having a relationship with God. This then leads to self-control (governing yourself) eating right, being on time, your talking, your walking, and your priorities, (saying no, where I need to say no); (saying yes, where I need to say yes); doing what needs to be done. Being disciplined in the practical things of life will have an effect in your spiritual life and you will become a person who can decide what you want to do, and then do it.

Many times we try to do more than what is possible. The people that seem to get things done, and are not all overwhelmed about it, are those who prepare ahead of time. When a proper preparation is done, then the actual doing whatever, seems easy. But when you wait until the task is at hand and make no preparation, it will seem like more than you can do. In fact, it is. Self-discipline makes all the difference. This means you do things (prepare) before they have to be done. This works in praying, in making meals, doing laundry, or paying bills. On and on the list could go. Self-discipline really is in everything in life, even getting up in the morning. Decide when you will get up, allow enough time for what you want to do, then go to bed accordingly. How much time do you need to sleep? This is governing yourself.

Self-control has nothing to do with making yourself read the Word. It comes through reading the Word. As we stick with it (perseverance), we will overcome into godliness - which flows into brotherly love and unconditional love. Whatever is going on in our lives, then becomes a practical influence on those around us. Self-control is just that!! Read Galatians 5 again.

The Promise: you will be fruitful and useful

The Condition: to work on having all these qualities increasing in your life.

Take time to memorize the verse. Write it on a card, carry it with you, repeat it many times a day. Also memorize the reference. Read II Peter 1:1-8, every day this week.
Let the word become flesh - a part of you!

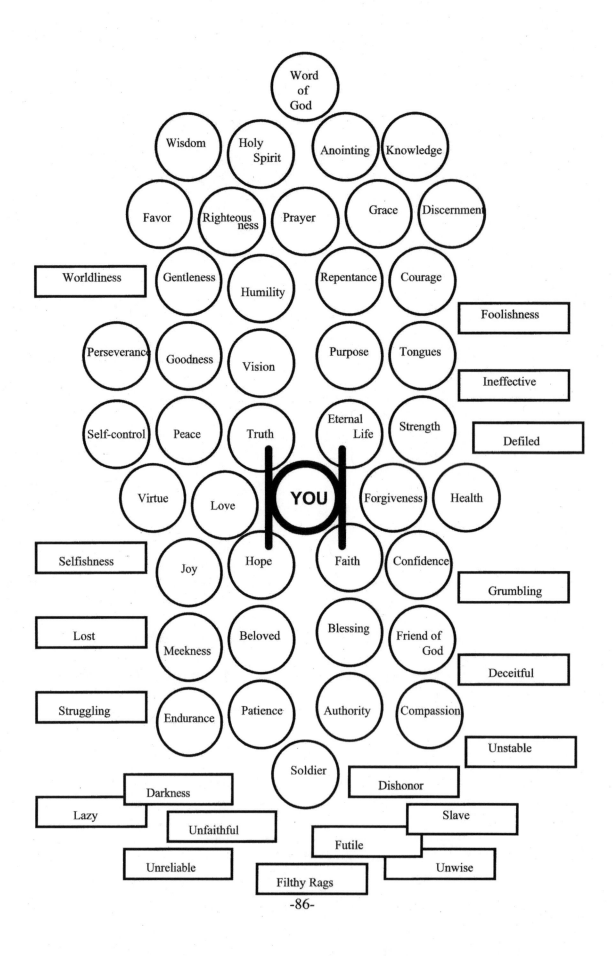

Perseverance

**I press on toward the goal
for the prize
of the upward call of God
in Christ Jesus
Philippians 3:14**

Perseverance, sticking to it, it's the way to get the job done. God has a lot of perseverance. "For I am confident of this very thing, that He who began a good work in you will perfect it until the day of Christ Jesus," Philippians 1:6. It means in simple words, not quitting until we have reached our goal.

The key is to have a goal to work for. When you start anything, decide what it is that you want to accomplish. Then if the first way doesn't work, try another. In order to solve a problem, you must have a vision, a working idea, a plan. Sometimes that plan doesn't work. Don't quit, but stop and try another plan. This is perseverance. People that accomplish great things in life, are people that failed many times, but they did not stop trying until they finished their vision.

This is what God does. If He is trying to teach you something, and you are not getting it, He will try another way. There is a song that talks about God making everything on earth in a week. "But He's still working on me." He is a very long-suffering and patient God.

Patience is a fruit (result) of walking in the Spirit. So is perseverance. Whatever is at hand to do, keep your eyes on the goal, the finished work, and you will be more patient to stay with it until it is done. When you look at life, and everything it brings as a vehicle with which to reach your final goal, it will bring you patience and motivate you to press on. For some people this comes easy, for others it is something you need to cultivate until you master it.

Notice here that perseverance comes after self-control. It is very hard to persevere if you do not have self-control working in your life. To change in these areas of your life you must start with small things. Doing something at a certain time of the day, maybe praying for a lost friend five minutes. If you fail to remember one day, try again. Don't give up.

The Promise: you will reach the goal, of every day, of every year, of your life.

The Condition: have a goal, receive a vision, (plan) work to accomplish it.

Take time to memorize the verse. Write it on a card, carry it with you, repeat it many times a day. Also memorize the reference. Read the entire chapter of Philippians 3, every day this week.
Let the word become flesh - a part of you!

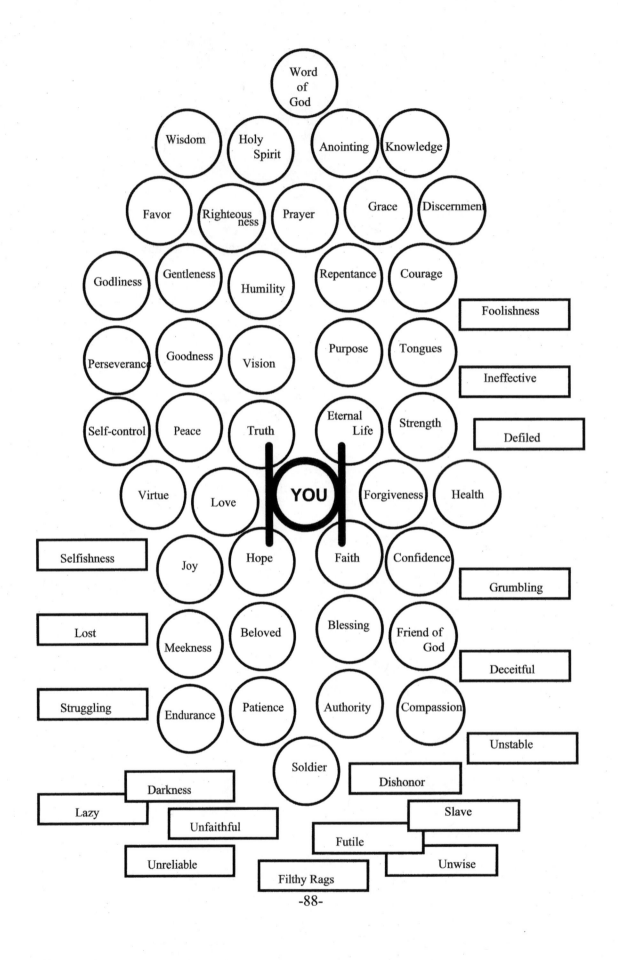

Godliness

**seeing that His divine power hath granted unto us
all things that pertain unto life and godliness,
through the knowledge of Him that called us
by his own glory and virtue;
II Peter 1:3**

Peter is writing to those who have received a faith of the same kind as his. A faith that is by the righteousness of our God and Saviour, Jesus Christ, (v.1). God's righteousness is first hearing the word, secondly thinking on it, and letting it come into our hearts. Then it becomes faith and we believe. The result of this being, God's righteousness. Only out of God's righteousness does godliness flow.

It is in the knowledge of God (knowing God) that we have grace and peace. In fact, Peter is saying," let grace and peace be multiplied to you." Multiplication causes abundance. When grace is at work in your life, you won't have to strive to try to make things work. They just work. Praying brings grace, this then brings peace. Peace is the heart cry of every person.

Peter laid it out very clear here that the Christian walk is a process. You cannot jump into godliness. It all begins with faith (believing), then virtue (thinking and acting properly), knowledge (getting to know God). Then we come to self-control (dealing with the flesh) (laying aside the old self, putting on the new self). As we work on that, perseverance follows. Perseverance simply means: not quitting, not giving up. Then comes godliness (being conformed to the image of Jesus, Ro.8). This is what our goal was to start with. In I Timothy 4:8-10, Paul teaches that godliness is something you should labor and strive for, because you have your hope fixed on the living God, who is the Savior of all men.

The divine power of God grants us everything we need for life and for godliness. That is a wonderful promise! Granted means: it has already been given to you. What has God given us? He has given us everything we will ever need for life and for godliness. It comes through the true knowledge of "Him who called us." True knowledge comes by: studying the Word, seeking His face, spending time with Him. This is a relationship, a relationship with God. As you walk in His promises (which are precious and magnificent) you become a partaker of His divine nature. In this way you escape the corruption which is in the world.

The Promise: an overcoming life

The Condition: acting on what we know, persevering in it, by faith.

Take time to memorize the verse. Write it on a card, carry it with you, repeat it many times a day. Also memorize the reference. Read the entire chapter of II Peter 1 every day this week.
Let the word become flesh - a part of you!

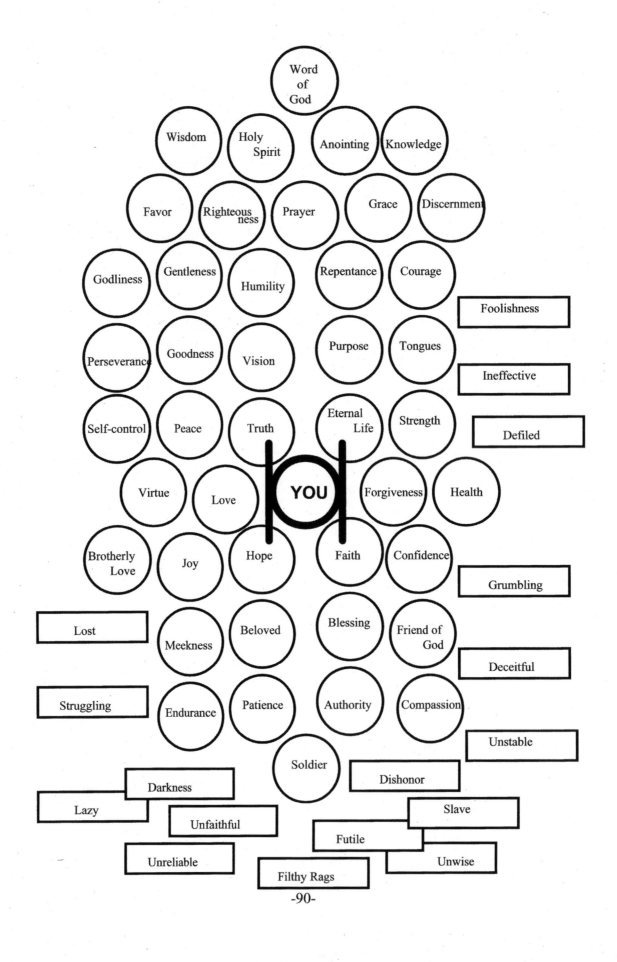

Brotherly Love

**"You shall love the Lord, your God
with all your Heart,
and with all your Soul,
and with all your Mind,
This is the great and foremost commandment,
The second is like it,
You shall love your neighbor as yourself
Matthew 22:37-39**

Brotherly love is conditional. It consists of you love me, and then I love you. You do something for me, then I do something for you. It's so much so that we call it being brotherly (sisterly). Jesus commanded us to love our neighbor as yourself. How much do you love yourself. Sometimes people get into their minds that it is godly to put themselves down, but it's not. God would want you to see the good in yourself. He is the one who made you. He made you exactly the way He wanted you to be.

How do you love yourself? When you love someone you want to know all about that person. You want to know his (her) desires, gifts, strengths and weaknesses. Really, you want to see them succeed. Don't become self-centered, but think about what your desires are. What is it that comes easy for you. This is what He would want you to do. He is the one who gave your gifts and talents to you.

May I let you in on a little secret though. Your gifts and talents usually need to be refined. This does not happen if you hide them. With trial and error, trying again and again, you can function in your gifts and talents that God placed within you in a way that you will make a difference in the world.

We all have a need to be needed, to make a difference. But when you first try, whatever it is, it is very easy to get upset with yourself and determine to never do it again. Use yourself like you would everyone else. Allow yourself to make mistakes, but at same time, keep it your goal to do the very best. Don't give up until you reach your goal.

The first and foremost commandment is: "to love the Lord with all your being." The second one being, "love your neighbor as yourself" They work together. As you love the Lord, and get to know Him, you then become acquainted with who you are, and then can also be a brother (sister) to your neighbor.

The Promise: your life will be fulfilled

The Condition: being obedient to the Word, living in reality

Take time to memorize the verse. Write it on a card, carry it with you, repeat it many times a day. Also memorize the reference. Read the entire chapter of Matthew 22 every day this week.
Let the word become flesh - a part of you!

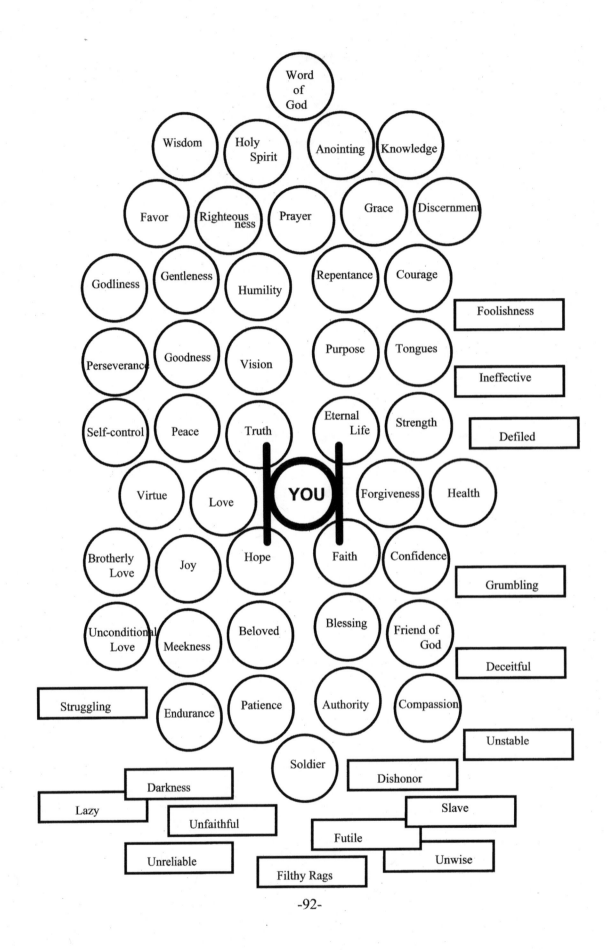

Unconditional Love

**For God so loved the world,
that he gave his only begotten Son,
that whosoever believeth on him
should not perish, but have eternal life.
John 3:16**

Unconditional love is just that. God loves us, not because of anything on our part. God loves every person that has ever been born, plus everyone that ever will be born. He loves us so much that He had a plan, how He would enable us to be at peace with Him, and have eternal life. He gave His Son, Jesus, to come and live as a man. He died for our sins, so that He might gave us eternal life. It is a gift, and nothing that we can earn. He did it all because He loves us so.

John 3:16 is still the greatest verse of all. This is the plan of God, that runs all through the Bible. God is very careful how He brings a concept to our attention the first time in His Word. It is something to watch for. The first time the word love is used is in Gen.22, when Abraham is to take his son, his only son who he loved, and offer him as a burnt offering. This is a perfect picture of what God the Father had in mind with his own Son.

The first time love is mentioned in the New Testament is in Matt.3:17 - "a voice from heaven 'This is My beloved Son, in whom I am well pleased." The second time, Mark 1:11 - "a voice from heaven saying, 'Thou art my Son, in whom I am well pleased." A third time, Luke 3:22 - " the Holy Ghost descended in a bodily shape like a dove upon him, and a voice from heaven, which said," Thou art my beloved Son, in thee I am well pleased." At last in John 3:16 - "For God so loved the world, that He gave His only begotten Son, that whosoever believeth in Him should not perish, but have everlasting life." Three times God shouts His love for His Son from heaven, then He tells us that He loved us, (yes us), so much that He was willing to sacrifice His only, beloved Son, in order that we might be saved.

It is so important that we know how much God loves us and to understand how important each one of us is to Him. When you understand the intense love of God toward you, it will forever change your outlook in life. He likes you, for He was the one who made you. He has a very special purpose in His mind concerning you. His love is not conditioned on what you have done or are doing.

The Promise: eternal life, the love of God flowing through you to others.

The Condition: believing that God gave His Son for you.

Take time to memorize the verse. Write it on a card, carry it with you, repeat it many times a day. Also memorize the reference. Read the entire chapter of John 3, every day this week.
Let the word become flesh - a part of you!

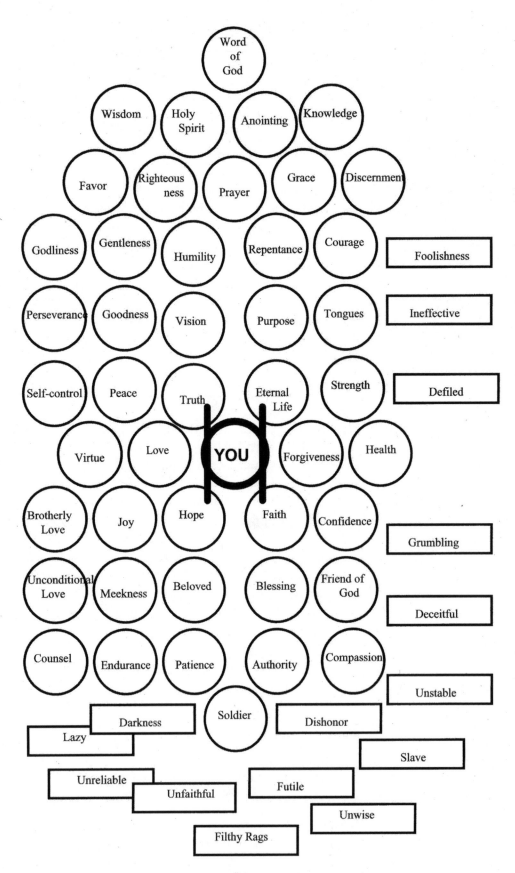

Sabbath Rest

There remains therefore - a Sabbath rest for the people of God
For the one who has entered His rest has himself
also rested from his works as God did from His
Let us therefore be diligent to enter that rest.
Hebrews 4:9,10,11a

The birth order of the children of Israel can be read about in Genesis 29 and 30. Jacob had children with two wives and their handmaidens. Leah and Rachel, (his wives) were always struggling with one another to be Jacob's favorite and to bear his children. Although we do not understand all this, we can get an understanding out of this for our lives. The names they gave their children expressed the feelings of their heart. It had an effect on their walk of life. Many years later, when the children of Israel were journeying through the wilderness in Numbers 10, God rearranged the order of the tribes. Judah was Leah's fourth son. When she gave birth to him she said," This time I will praise the Lord," Genesis 29:35. She quit bearing children at that time. In the tribe order Judah (Praise) was to go first.

Later Leah had two more sons, Issachar and Zebulum. Only after Rachel's handmaiden (30:5,7) and her own handmaiden (30:10,12) each bore Jacob two sons. When Issachar was born she felt it was a reward, and she came into a rest within herself (30:18). In the tribe order, the tribe of Issachar was to march second. When Zebulum was born, (30:20) she felt her husband would now honor her. When Jacob blessed his sons (49:13), he talked about Zebulum living by the seashore and becoming a haven for ships. He was to be a lighthouse for those on the sea. (This happened after the Israelites entered the Promised Land.) In the tribe order, they were to march third.

This is the way God also orders our lives. Praise needs to be first. This is ministering to the Lord. Then we must come into a Sabbath rest of God. When God created the earth, He worked for six days, then He rested, Genesis 2:2. This was a Sabbath rest. Rest comes as a reward after an accomplishment. Leah worked through the struggles with her sister, and came into a rest. So you also will come into a Sabbath rest, when you have worked through your struggles. Third, we will be a lighthouse for those who need a safe haven from the sea of life. Many sailors have been saved, because they saw the light of a lighthouse.

The Promise: many will come to you for counsel, as sailors come to a lighthouse

The Condition: Let praise be a part of your life; work through your struggles and enter into a Sabbath rest with God. Then you will become a lighthouse.

Take time to memorize the verse. Write it on a card, carry it with you, repeat it many times a day. Also memorize the reference. Read the entire chapter of Hebrews 4, every day this week.
Let the word become flesh - a part of you!

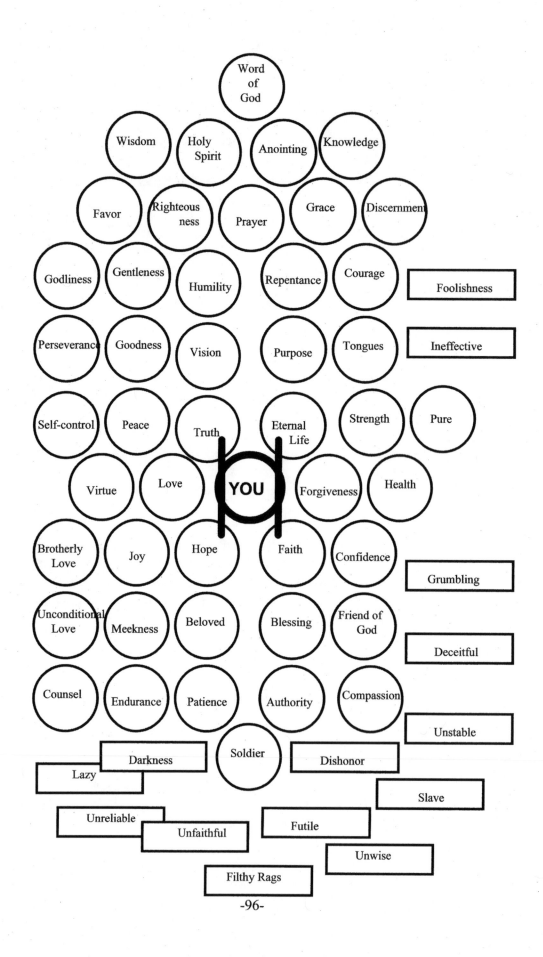

Pure

To the pure all things are pure,
but to those who are
defiled and unbelieving
nothing is pure
but both their mind
and their conscience are defiled.
Titus 1:15

Titus is a small book written by Paul, to Titus. It will not take you long to read it. But it is so packed full of how to live a pure life, that if you study in it, you will study for a long time. Pure means: not mixed, clean. We are to have clean hands, and a pure heart, cleansed by the Blood. In this same verse it talks about those who are defiled and unbelieving. To such nothing is pure.

The first chapter tells us what is required of an overseer (elder), (v.6-9). An elder must be above reproach. Above reproach means, there is nothing to blame about a person, no shame or disgrace. He then goes on to explain how to do that, what must be in his life, and what he needs to cleanse himself of. Don't think because you might not be an "elder" this does not speak to you. This list I find profitable for all, a way to be pure.

When we live in purity, our heart is set on our Lord. We will serve Him with our whole heart, it will not be a side line. Notice (v.6), first he talks about the state of his family. Then (v.7) is about his attitude, (v.8) reaching out to others and good character. Lastly then, (v.9) his ministry. After going through (v.10-14) saying what kind of men that need to be silenced, he added this verse, "to the pure all things are pure."

To live above reproach can only be attained if we live a life that has no secrets. We don't need to tell everybody, everything, this is wisdom. But, let your deeds and thoughts be so that you could share them with anyone. Ask the Holy Spirit what He would want you to share, and with whom. This is not difficult, it's rather simple. If it's not something just anyone could know, don't do it. Don't even think about it. Ask God to cleanse you from its' desire. Set your goal to be pure in your mind and in your conscience. To be defiled and unbelieving is, "professing to know God, but by their deeds they deny Him, "(v.16). A person that's just talk, not doing what they talk.

The Promise: being able to walk above reproach

The Condition: desiring purity

Take time to memorize the verse. Write it on a card, carry it with you, repeat it many times a day. Also memorize the reference. Read the entire chapter of Titus 1, every day this week.
Let the word become flesh - a part of you!

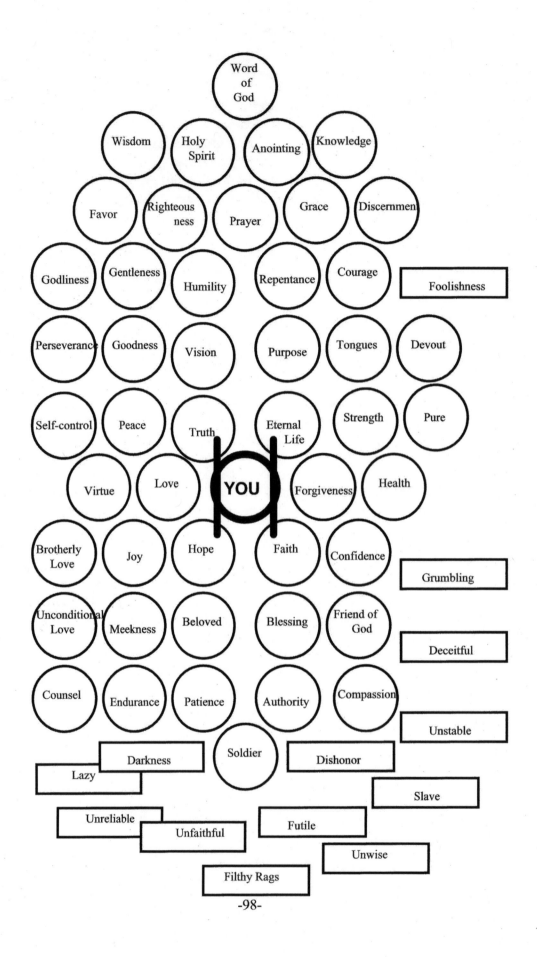

Devout

**These things speak and exhort
and reprove with all authority.
Let no one disregard you.
Titus 2:15**

Let us continue our study of Titus. "For the grace of God has appeared, bringing salvation to all men,"
(v.11). Salvation instructed us, "to live sensibly, righteously, and godly."
We are to "speak the things which are fitting for sound doctrine," (v.1). He gave us this list:
Older men are to be: (v.2)   1) temperate   2) dignified   3) sensible
                                   4) sound in faith   5) sound in love   6) sound in perseverance
Older women are to be: (v.3) 1) reverent in their behavior   2) teaching what is good
They are to encourage the young women: (v.4,5) 1) to love their husbands
        2) to love their children   3) to be sensible   4) pure   5) workers at home   6) kind
        7) to be subject to their own husbands   " that the word of God may not be dishonored."
Urge young men to be: (v.6)   1) sensible   2) be an example of good deeds (in all things)
        3) pure in doctrine   4) dignified   5) sound in speech - beyond reproach
            "that the opponent may be put to shame," (v.8).
Urge bondslaves to be: (v.9)   1) subject to their own masters (in everything)
        2) be well-pleasing (not argumentative)   3) not stealing   4) showing good faith
            "that they may adorn the doctrine of God our Savior in every respect."

These are the things we are to speak, to exhort, to reprove with all authority. Jesus has all authority,
Matthew 28:18. When we go in His Name we function in that authority.

Remind them (all) to be: (3:1-2) 1) subject to rulers 2) subject to authority 3) obedient 4) ready for
        very good deed 5) speak evil of no one 6) uncontentious 7) gentle 8) considerate to all

We were not saved on the basis of righteous deeds, but through the kindness of God and His mercy,
(3:5). Jesus richly poured out the Holy Spirit upon us, so that we might have a hope of eternal life. He
wants us to speak very confidently about this, "so that those who have believed God may be careful to
engage in good deeds" (3:8).

The Promise: you will become a person that people want to follow

The Condition: first live, then speak, exhort and reprove the things spoken of in Titus.

Take time to memorize the verse. Write it on a card, carry it with you, repeat it many times a day.
Also memorize the reference. Read the chapters of Titus 2,3, every day this week.
Let the word become flesh - a part of you!

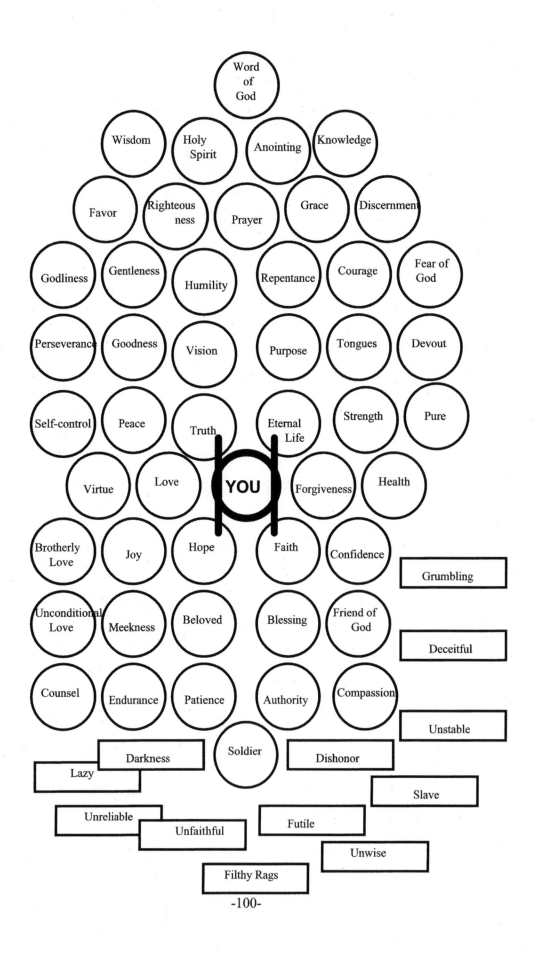

Fear of God

**The fear of the Lord is
the beginning of knowledge;
Fools despise
wisdom and instruction.
Proverbs 1:7**

The correct fear of the Lord is not being afraid of Him. Rather, it means to respect and honor Him, to see Him as One to trust and obey, to submit to His ways. He is King. As Americans we do not understand how a king operates. Kings set laws for their lands and the people do not have a voice in it. There is no way to change them, they must be obeyed. The laws of God will never change, you need to respect and honor them. The more you get to know God, the more you will respect and honor Him. Every principle of God is for your good and protection. His desire is for you.

He is Lord. He has made a way for us. Man cannot save himself, but needs a Savior. Neither can we provide for ourselves. He has made provision for everything we need in life. Trust Him for your life. Know that in Him is everything you may ever need. He is a Shepherd. He leads us. God is so good. He says in, Hebrews 13:5, "He will never leave us, nor forsake us." He is always leading, whether in a valley or on a mountain top. Be courageous and follow Him.

He is holy. He can not look on sin. We come to Him in Christ Jesus. Jesus has total victory. When He said, "it is finished," it was finished. The debt of sin was settled. He also overcame death. He arose, and is with the Father. He hears and sees. God hears the cries of our heart. He hears every plead we make. They (the cries) come to Him through Jesus Christ, the holy One. He looks down upon us. It is in Christ Jesus that He sees us. He sees us victorious and holy, justified (just-as-if-I-had-never-sinned).

He understands. He is all-knowing. He knows your every thought, and the motives of your heart. He knows your frame. He is mindful that we are but dust, Psalms 103:14. He knows about every fear you have. He is greater than any danger you might ever encounter. Release it to Him. He understands. Yes, when no one seems to understand, God still does. He understands you. There are no secrets with Him. Luke 12:3, "Whatever you have said in the dark, shall be said in the light, What you have whispered in the inner rooms shall be proclaimed on the housetops."

The Promise: knowledge and wisdom

The Condition: building a relationship with God

Take time to memorize the verse. Write it on a card, carry it with you, repeat it many times a day. Also memorize the reference. Read the entire chapter of Proverbs 1, every day this week.
Let the word become flesh - a part of you!

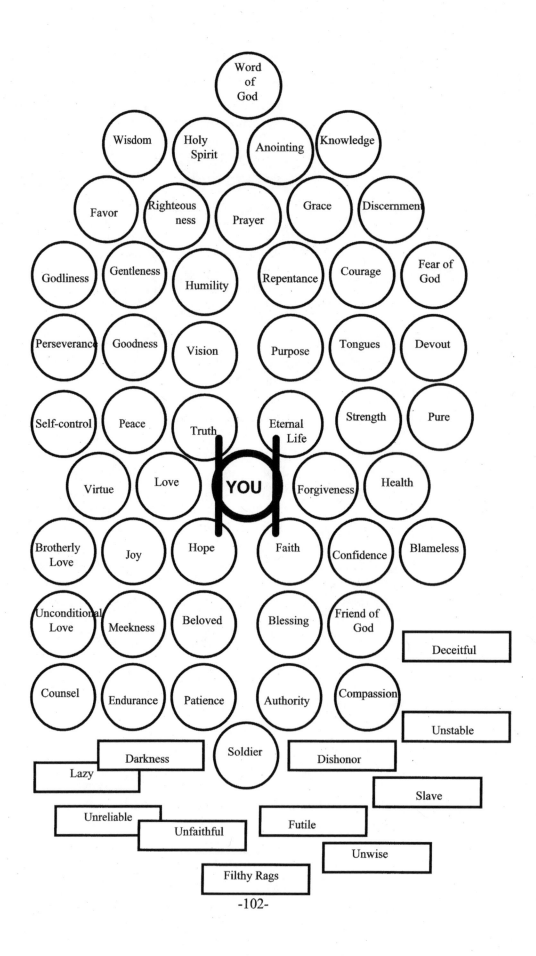

Blameless

Do all things without grumbling or disputing
that you may prove yourselves
to be blameless and innocent
children of God - above reproach
Phillipians.2:14-15

Blameless and innocence can only be attained when you deal with every situation from the tree of Life. No matter how awful the issue is, there is a way to redeem it, when you do not point the accusing finger. You may say that you are not a person who complains. Check your heart, does it complain? What is the first thought that comes to you, in an inconvenient circumstance? Is it a thought of dread, self-pity or anger? Or are you thinking of getting even. It could be that you are in utter defeat. Stop! What would Jesus do? Remember, I Corinthians 10:13, there is always a correct solution to every problem.

You alone, are responsible for the decisions you make. Therefore, you cannot say, "but they made me say or do thus and thus." First of all ask yourself, "Is this my decision to make?" If it is something you need to make a decision about, don't put it off. If it's not, then don't make it, even when people might want you to. Leave the matter unsettled. You have responded by making a decision, that the decision is not yours to make.

You need to respond to everything that comes your way. God will give you grace for what you are responsible for. There is no grace given where you don't have responsibility. Where you have stepped in and taken responsibility that was not yours, you most likely will get frustrated and grumble and complain. The tree of Life brings restoration to the situation. Ask yourself, "How can I help the person (people) to be restored in this matter?" It will make a difference in how you respond.

Take time to reflect, "Did anything change because I know about the matter?" Take time to work it through. Many times it's good to pray about the situation until you have direction on how to proceed. If you do this with the issues where it is possible, God will also answer your split second prayers, "Help, Lord" in momentary places.

The Promise: God will work in you, both to will and to work His good pleasure in you and then you will be blameless. You will always know how to respond.

The Condition: do nothing from selfishness or empty conceit, but with humility of mind let each of you regard one another as more important than himself (v.3)

Take time to memorize the verse. Write it on a card, carry it with you, repeat it many times a day. Also memorize the reference. Read the entire chapter of Philippians 2, every day this week.
Let the word become flesh - a part of you!

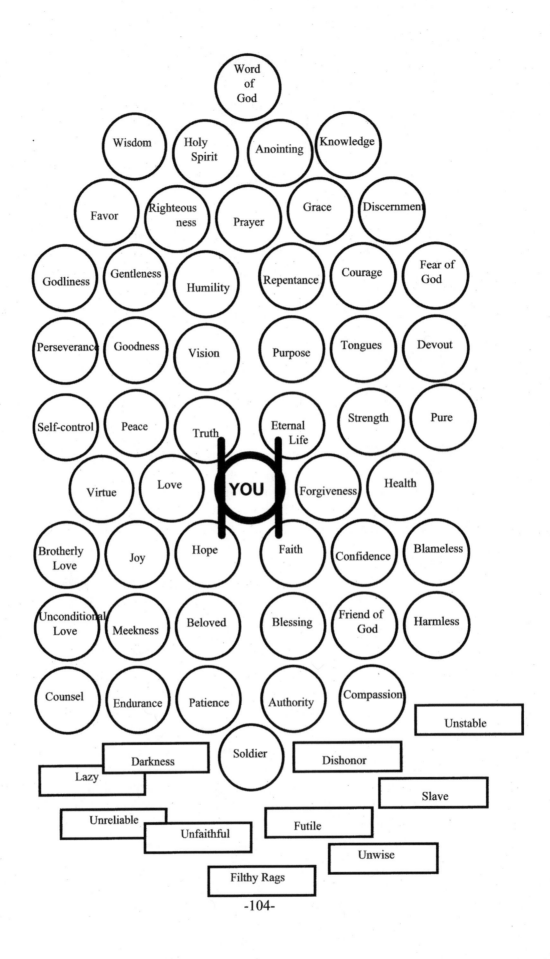

Harmless

**Behold, I send you out as sheep
in the midst of wolves,
be ye therefore wise as serpents,
and harmless as doves.
Matthew 10:16**

When Jesus sent out His 12 disciples, He gave them authority. He also told them what the authority was for. "Preach," He said, "the kingdom of heaven is at hand." Then He said, "heal the sick, raise the dead, cleanse the leper, cast out demons, freely you have received, freely give." That is what He gave them authority for. The authority given by Jesus is still for the same purpose, to minister good to others. When we use it in this way, we will be harmless.

As you go about doing God's work, praying for those in need, giving freely what God has given you, you must always remember, there are wolves (people with evil intentions) out there. These people will take what you are trying to accomplish and turn it around to something quite different. A wolf will sneak around in the shadows silently until he sees his prey at a vulnerable moment, then he jumps on it. His aim is to kill. This really is the plan of the enemy and he uses people to get his job done.

A serpent is always alert. In Matthew 7:24 we read, a wise man is one who reads the Word and acts on it. To be a wise person you must do the same. As you read the Word, and the Holy Spirit speaks to you how that will apply to your life, listen to what He is saying. See the good in everything, but stay alert. Know who your real enemy is. The Devil, your enemy is out to trip you up.

A dove is an animal that is totally harmless. They will fly anywhere. They don't seem to be easily scared. How can we be like that? Keep in mind who sent you, and always see the good in those around you. Every person has good in them, it does not matter how hard it is for you to see that. God has put good in each person. Many times it's lying dormant. As you tell them about the good you see, they become a new person.

God loves us all, He wants every person in the whole world to come back home to Him. He wants us all to be of use in His Kingdom on earth. By gently speaking to sinners, seeing good in them, you can touch their lives. You can go where others can not.

The Promise: the sick will be healed, the dead will arise, lepers cleanse and the demons will flee.

The Condition: go with Jesus' authority, be alert and wise, but very gentle and harmless

Take time to memorize the verse. Write it on a card, carry it with you, repeat it many times a day. Also memorize the reference. Read the entire chapter of Matthew 10, every day this week.
Let the word become flesh - a part of you!

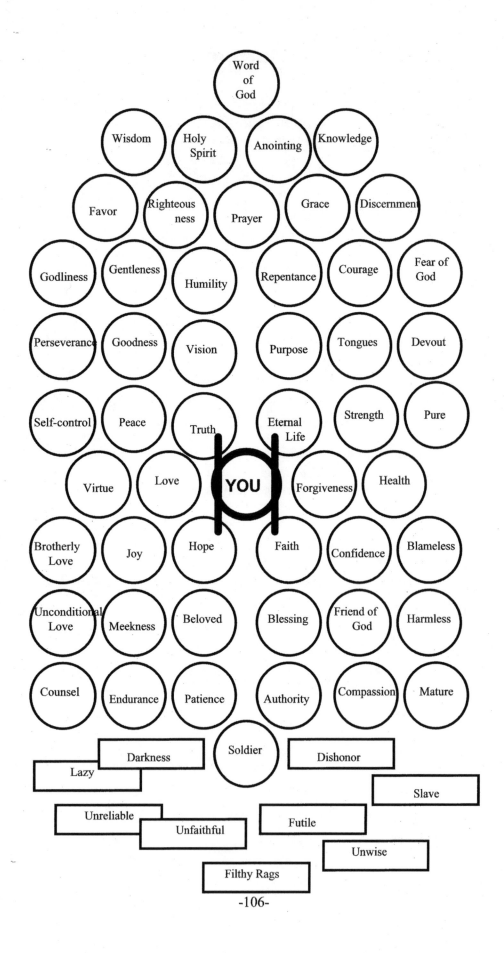

Word
of
God

Wisdom

Holy
Spirit

Anointing

Knowledge

Favor

Righteous
ness

Prayer

Grace

Discernment

Godliness

Gentleness

Humility

Repentance

Courage

Fear of
God

Perseverance

Goodness

Vision

Purpose

Tongues

Devout

Self-control

Peace

Truth

Eternal
Life

Strength

Pure

Virtue

Love

YOU

Forgiveness

Health

Brotherly
Love

Joy

Hope

Faith

Confidence

Blameless

Unconditional
Love

Meekness

Beloved

Blessing

Friend of
God

Harmless

Counsel

Endurance

Patience

Authority

Compassion

Mature

Darkness

Soldier

Dishonor

Lazy

Slave

Unreliable

Unfaithful

Futile

Unwise

Filthy Rags

Mature

but speaking the truth in love,
we are to grow up in all aspects into Him
who is the head even Christ.
Ephesians 4:15

To be mature, we must remain teachable. Christ ascended to heaven, He took captive a host of captives and gave gifts to men. He gave apostles, prophets, evangelists, pastors and teachers to the body of Christ (the Church). As you remain open to hear what they have to say, you will become a mature person. A mature person is not one who knows it all, but one who is ever ready to know more.

Chapter four starts out by telling us we should walk worthy of our calling. People ponder long on the question, what is my calling? What would God want me to do? Your calling is made up in many small ways. I Thessalonians 5:16-18, "rejoice always, pray without ceasing, in everything give thanks; for this is God's will for you in Christ Jesus." This pertains to everyone.

Then there are things about yourself that you cannot change. Are you a man or a woman? Where were you born? etc. These were not mistakes, but when taken into consideration will help you understand the call of God on your life. Going back to Romans 12, which we studied in Goodness, he shared of the motivational gifts (v.6-8). God has given each person a gift which motivates (drives) them. Here in chapter 12, they are named, 1) prophecy, 2) helps, 3) teacher, 4) exhorter, 5) giving, 6) organizer, 7) mercy. We do not have room to expand on these, but it will help you tremendously to study these, and see what has been placed within you by God. This will greatly help you to understand your calling. Don't try to be like someone else, but understand what is within yourself and flow in that.

You have a part to play in the body of Christ. God does not only want you to become mature, but He wants the body of Christ to come into maturity. As each person grows up in Christ and everyone works together in the body of Christ, we will become a mature body, (Church). Studying the book of Ephesians will help you to grow up in Christ.

The Promise: becoming a mature person

The Condition: humility, submitting to the unchangeables in your life, facing truth, always being ready to learn

You now are surrounded with 51 mighty Blessings, four carrying you, fourteen going before you , five coming behind and fourteen on either side. Do not stop here, but place nine more blessings to follow.

Take time to memorize the verse. Write it on a card, carry it with you, repeat it many times a day. Also memorize the reference. Read Ephesians 4:1-16, every day this week.
Let the word become flesh - a part of you!

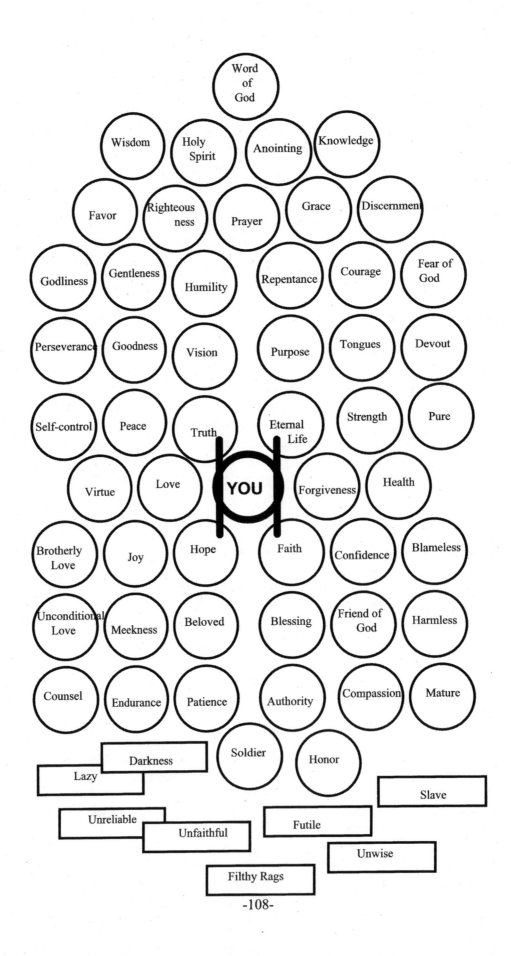

Honor

If anyone serves Me, let him follow Me.
and where I am, there shall My servant also be.
if anyone serves Me, the Father will honor him
John 12:26

Jesus spoke this right after He had been honored. Proverbs 15:33, "The fear of the Lord is the instruction for wisdom. And before honor comes humility." Jesus had fulfilled this proverb. He had humbled Himself, by riding on a donkey. The crowd honored Him. Isaiah 43, (v.1), God says "do not fear, for I have redeemed you, I have called you by name, you are Mine." Then in (v.4), "Since you are precious in My sight. Since you are honored and I love you." This is the Lord speaking to His children.

In Hebrews 2:6-9, we read how God honored man when He created him. He crowned him with glory and honor. God appointed him over everything He had made. Adam and Eve lost this on the day they sinned. Jesus again is "crowned with glory and honor, because of the suffering of death."

Jesus was honored by God at different times. I Peter 1:17, Peter says that Jesus, "received honor and glory from God the Father," when they were on the Mount of Transfiguration, Matthew 17. This is what God said, "This is My Beloved Son with whom I am well-pleased." In Matthew 3:17, at His baptism, God from heaven had spoken the same thing, and here in John 12:28, He again honors Him. This is right after riding into Jerusalem on a donkey.

Honor is a special respect that is given to a person. We are commanded to honor the following:
John 5:23 - we are to "honor the Son, even as we honor the Father"
Hebrews 13:4 - "let the marriage be held in honor among all"
I Peter 3:7 - "husband grant her (his wife) honor as a fellow heir of the grace of God,"
       "so that your prayers may not be hindered."
Ephesians 6:2 - "honor your father and mother" (v.3) "that it may be well with you, and that you
       may live long on earth."
I Timothy 5:3 - " honor widows who are widows indeed"
I Timothy 5:17 - "let the elders who rule well be considered worthy of double honor."
Romans 12:10 - "give preference to one another in honor"
I Peter 2:7 - "honor all men, love the brotherhood, fear God, honor the king."

The Promise: God the Father will honor you

The Condition: serve Jesus, and follow Him, humble yourself, honor others

Take time to memorize the verse. Write it on a card, carry it with you, repeat it many times a day. Also memorize the reference. Read the entire chapter of John 12, every day this week.
Let the word become flesh - a part of you!

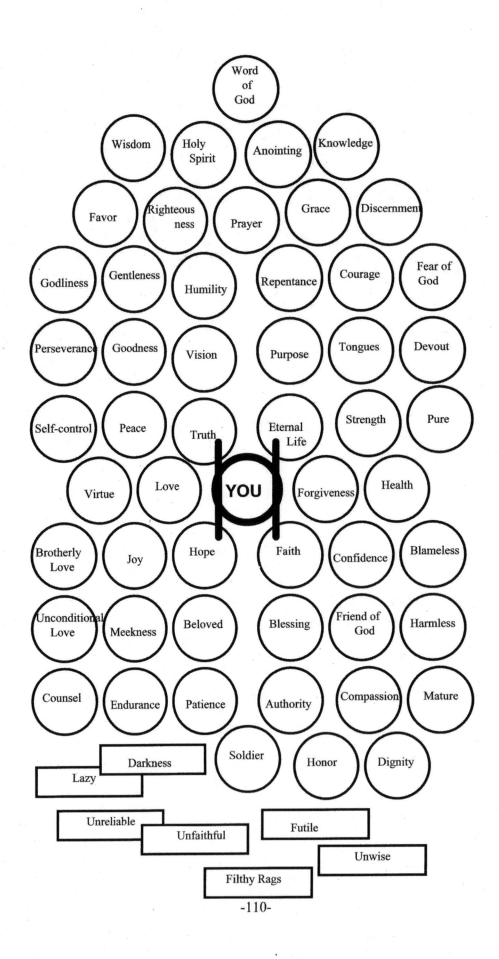

Dignity

**And hath made us kings and priests
unto God and His Father;
to Him be glory and dominion
for ever and ever, Amen.
Revelation 1:6 K.J.**

The book of Revelation was written by the apostle John when he was an aged man. It is a revelation of Jesus Christ, written to His bond-servants, (v.1). He wrote what he saw, and said that those who read it and heed to the things that were written would be blessed, (v.3). A bond-servant is one who was set free in the year of Jubilee, but chose to remain and serve his master. He wrote it to the seven churches in Asia, proclaiming peace and grace from the seven Spirits around His throne, and from Jesus Christ. This letter is now written to us from those in heaven! He describes Jesus as, "a faithful witness, the first-born of the dead, and the ruler of the kings of earth. And He has made us kings and priests unto His God and Father."

A king is one who rules over those under him. He makes decisions and takes responsibility for the decisions he makes. This was the mandate that God gave Adam, Genesis 1:28. God blessed Adam saying, "Be fruitful and multiply, and fill the earth, and subdue it." He was "to rule over the fish of the sea and over the birds of the sky, and over every living thing that moves on the earth." Everything that was on earth was given to him so that he could direct and take care of it, (v.28-30). When Adam sinned he gave this authority to the enemy of our soul, the Devil. But verse six of Revelation 1 tells us, when Jesus released us from our sins by His blood, He has re-enstated to us the mandate given to Adam.

A priest is one who ministers to God, one who talks with Him. In Exodus 28:41, the priests were to be clothed in priestly garments, then Aaron was to anoint, ordain, and consecrate them, "that they may serve Me as priests." As we clothe ourselves in God's principles, He will anoint, ordain, and consecrate us for each day.

A dignitary is a person with high rank. To walk with dignity, you must know who you are in Christ. To continue on in humility you must remember, it is in Christ. Then lift your head and walk as a king and a priest would, choose royalty.

The Promise: a God-confidence in you - that will cause the people around you to respect you.

The Condition: to chose to become a bond-servant of the Lord Jesus Christ, know that in the eyes of God, you are a king and you are a priest, a child of God.

Take time to memorize the verse. Write it on a card, carry it with you, repeat it many times a day. Also memorize the reference. Read the entire chapter of Revelation 1, every day this week.
Let the word become flesh - a part of you!

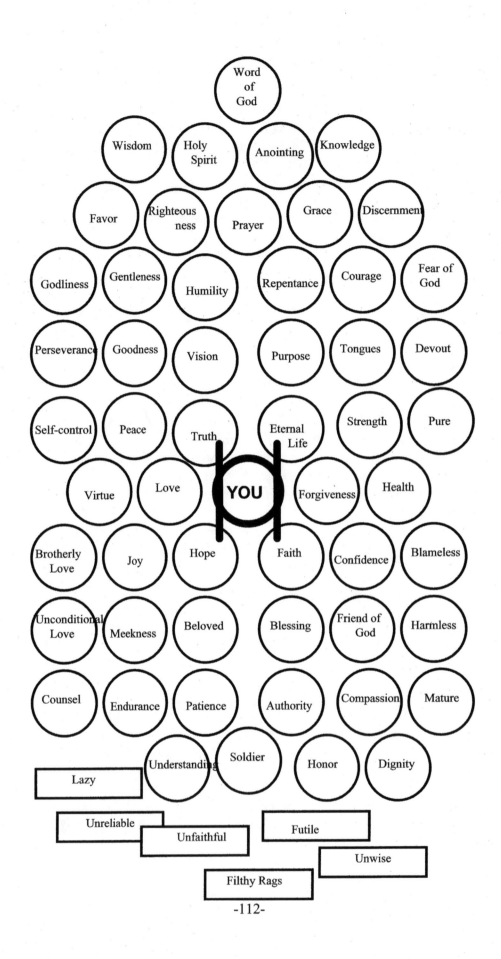

Understanding

so that Christ may dwell in your hearts through faith;
and that you being rooted and grounded in love,
may be able to comprehend with all the saints
what is the breadth and length and height and depth,
and to know the love of Christ - which surpasses knowledge,
that you may be filled up to all the fullness of God.
Ephesians 3:17-19

Understanding is the difference between light and darkness, Matthew 6:23. Understanding happens when "the eyes of your heart become enlightened," Ephesians 1:18. Understanding is knowing in your heart. You can know the love of God in your mind, and still not understand it.

Verse 14 through 20 is a prayer. It is directed to God the Father, asking Him to grant you "to be strengthened with power through His Spirit, (Holy Spirit) in the inner man. "So that" (you need this to prepare yourself), "Christ may dwell in your hearts through faith" then "you will be rooted and grounded in love" (v.17) and also then "you will be able to comprehend" (understand) all the dimensions of Christ, (v.18). "And to know the love of Christ, which surpasses knowledge." (this is more than knowing how big the love of Christ is in your mind, it is understanding it with your heart). "That you may be filled up to all the fullness of God," (v.19). We may ask all this, but then (v.20), He is able to do more, "exceedingly, abundantly, beyond all that we ask or think." What an understanding! This can only be understood with your heart.

As you read through Ephesians 3, notice that God has given us understanding in an area which has been hidden in all ages past. That the Gentiles are also fellow heirs, fellow members of the body, fellow partakers of the promise in Christ Jesus through the gospel, (v.6).

God let us in on His eternal purpose, (v.10). Through the church, "the manifold wisdom of God, (is to) be made known, to the rulers and the authorities in heavenly places." Because of Christ, Satan's kingdom has fallen, but it is still ruling in the hearts of those who have not received God's love in their hearts. We, the church, need to make known to him what Christ did for mankind. We need to cast him down, in prayer, Ephesians 6:10-18.

The Promise: learning to know God

The Condition: understanding with your heart, not only your mind.

Take time to memorize the verse. Write it on a card, carry it with you, repeat it many times a day. Also memorize the reference. Read the entire chapter of Ephesians 3, every day this week.
Let the word become flesh - a part of you!

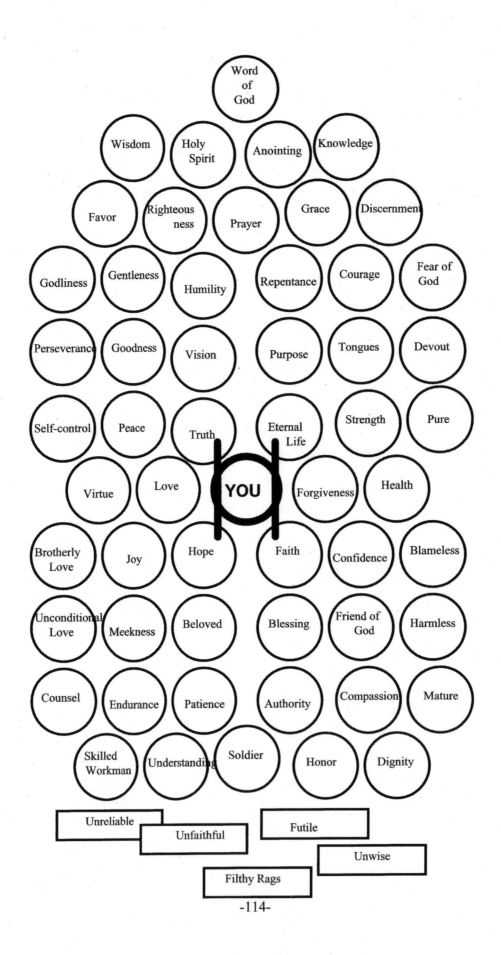

Skilled Workman

Whatever you do, do your work heartily,
as for the Lord rather than for men.
Colossians 3:23

As you read through Colossians 3 notice the outline of putting off the old self and putting on the new self. This is the only way to be able to be a skilled workman. When you have things in your life, that weigh down on you, you cannot do as a good of a job in whatever you are doing. But if you have the blessings of God walking before you, coming along beside you, and following you, you will be able to excel in all you set yourself to accomplish.

Know your position with Christ at all times, set your mind on things above. For (v.3) "you have died and your life is hidden with Christ in God." Paul says, "consider the members of your earthly body as dead to......" (v.5) and these are things which have been mentioned before. But search your heart about these issues. But now he says, " also put them all aside," and he named some more ...., (v.8).

The key to this is to replace an old character with a godly one. First (v.12) you need to realize that you have been chosen by God, that you are holy and beloved. Then the things you put on are just what you have been doing here in this study. "Put on a heart of compassion, kindness, humility, gentleness, and patience, forgiveness, love, peace and thankfulness" (v.12 through 14). If you need refreshing in any of these, take time to go back and do that.

The key to unlock all of this in your life is (v.16). "Let the word of Christ richly dwell within you with all wisdom, teaching and admonishing one another with psalms, hymns and spiritual songs, singing with thankfulness in your hearts to God." Doing everything in the name of the Lord Jesus, and whatever you cannot do or say in the name of Jesus, do not do it.

Verses 18, 19, 20, 21, and 22 are very straight forth directions on how to conduct your lives in the relationships of every day life. Luke 16:10 fits so well. It all starts out with the smallest things in your lives. When you do these small things as unto the Lord, you will also do the big things as unto Him. Really there are no big things. Everything is made up of a series of little things and it makes all the difference in the preparation you have given it, see self-control page 85.

The Promise: a reward of God's inheritance (v.24)

The Condition: take off your old self, put on the new self, set your mind on things above.

Take time to memorize the verse. Write it on a card, carry it with you, repeat it many times a day. Also memorize the reference. Read the entire chapter of Colossians 3, every day this week.
Let the word become flesh - a part of you!

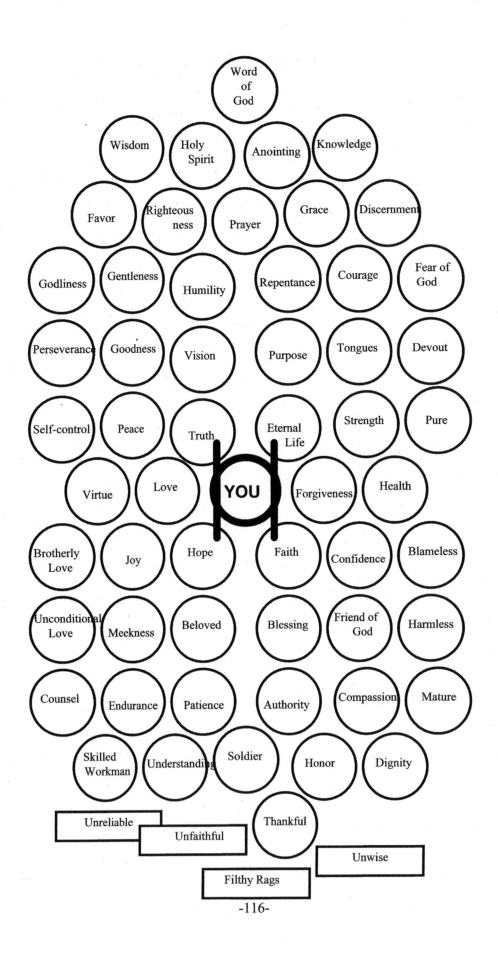

Thankful

Rejoice always,
Pray without ceasing
in everything give thanks
for this is; God's will for you
in Christ Jesus.
I Thessalonians 5:16-18

"For everything created by God is good and nothing is to be rejected, if it is received with gratitude, for it is sanctified by means of the Word of God and prayer," I Timothy 4:4,5. Being thankful is a heart issue. When we humble ourselves and acknowledge that we can do nothing of ourselves, it's because of God's provision that anything comes about. He provides the air we breathe, the water we drink. "He causes His sun to rise on the evil and the good, and sends rain on the righteous and the unrighteous," Matthews 5:45. We are here as stewards, to take care of the many things God has provided.

We just naturally do a good job caring for what we cherish and appreciate. The more we can realize the importance and the value of everything around us, the more grateful we will be. I think of a song, "Give thanks with a grateful heart, give thanks to the Holy One, Give thanks, because He has given Jesus Christ, His Son. And now let the weak say, 'I'm strong.' Let the poor say, 'I am rich.' Because of what the Lord has done for us, give thanks." Everything we accomplish is because of Him, let us never forget that.

In Romans 1, Paul writes about what happens when people do not give thanks to God, men that suppress the truth in unrighteousness, (v.18). He says, "God's invisible attributes, His eternal power and divine nature have been clearly seen, being understood through what was made, so that they have no excuse," (v.20). This is what happens, "they do not honor Him as God, or give thanks," and "they become futile in their speculations and their foolish hearts are darkened," (v.21).

Verses 19-22 of I Thessalonians 5 then, gives us some do not's. Which all then leads up to (v.23), "may the God of peace, Himself sanctify you entirely; and may your spirit and soul and body be preserved complete, without blame at the coming of our Lord Jesus Christ. " God has made a way, He has a perfect plan. When we grasp that, it's not hard to be thankful at all.

The Promise: as you become a grateful, thankful person, you will also become a good steward

The Condition: rejoice always, pray without ceasing, in everything give thanks, seeing God in all things

Take time to memorize the verse. Write it on a card, carry it with you, repeat it many times a day. Also memorize the reference. Read the entire chapter of I Thessalonians 5, every day this week. **Let the word become flesh - a part of you!**

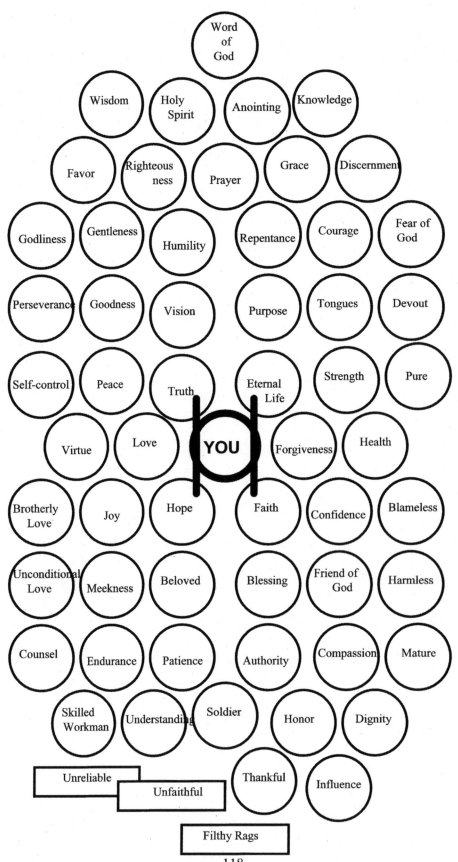

Influence

Therefore, be careful how you walk,
not as unwise men, but as wise,
making the most of your time,
because the days are evil.
So then do not be foolish,
but understand what the will of the Lord is.
Ephesians 5:15-17

As you walk through this life you are an influence to those around you. Psalms 90:12, "So teach us to number our days, that we may present to Thee a heart of wisdom." When this journey of life you are on will end, what is it you want to leave behind for those who follow you ?

As you place God's blessings around yourself, you become a godly influence, imitators of God (v.1). You now have 57 blessings traveling with you. Four to carry you, fourteen going ahead of you, fourteen on either side and eleven following you. Think about it. Are they all in tact as you would want them to be? Don't allow any one of these to be missing.

Ephesians 5, says that to be an imitator of God you are to walk in love, to be an offering and a sacrifice to God as a fragrant aroma. It smells good to God when you walk in this way, but it also smells good to the people around you. Don't you like to be around a person who walks in love? The things you do have an effect on those who follow, (v.3). It is not fitting to have a lot of loose talk, but rather a giving of thanks, (v.1). For no immoral, impure or covetous person has an inheritance in the kingdom of Christ and God, (v.5).

Then He shares that it is so important what we "hear". We hear many things as we go through a day. But the things we really hear are what we believe. Everything our ear hears we screen through our belief system, then we throw out what does not agree with it. Verse ten sums it all up, "trying to learn what is pleasing to the Lord." We want to walk as children of light. The fruit of light consists of goodness, righteousness, and truth. When we walk in light, we can hide nothing. Our walk and all we do is open for all to see. Our walk talks louder than our talk talks.

The Promise: receiving a heart of wisdom that can understand what the will of the Lord is

The Condition: be filled with the spirit, speaking good things to one another, your heart filled with praise, "always giving thanks for all things in the name of our Lord Jesus Christ to God the Father; and be subject to one another in the fear of Christ," (v.18-20).

Take time to memorize the verse. Write it on a card, carry it with you, repeat it many times a day. Also memorize the reference. Read Ephesians 5:1- 21, every day this week.
Let the word become flesh - a part of you!

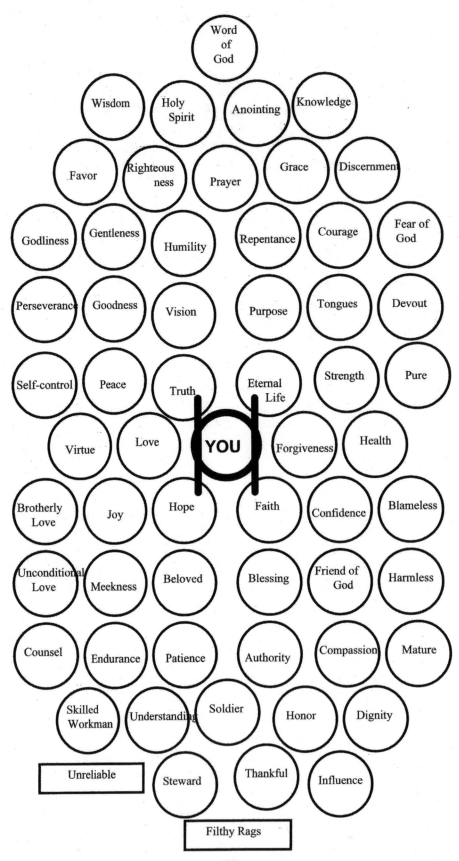

Steward

**He who is faithful in what is least,
is faithful also in much,
and he who is unjust in what is least
is unjust also in much
Luke 16:10**

Being a steward is a matter of taking care of something. Being a good steward is a matter of being faithful, of taking the responsibility of doing it right. In Luke 16, the master praised the unjust steward of making a shrewd decision, (v.8). In Matthew 25:14-30, we read an account of a master and his slaves. He entrusted his possessions to them (v.14), each according to their ability. When he came back to settle accounts with them, listen to what he said. To the first two (v.21) (v.23), he said, "Well done, good and faithful slave, you were faithful with a few things, I will put you in charge of many things, enter into the joy of your master."

But to the third one, he said, "You wicked, lazy slave, take away from him what he has, give it to the first one." This slave was afraid to do anything. Jesus added (v.29) "For to everyone who has shall more be given, and he shall have an abundance; but from the one who does not have, even what he does have shall be taken from him." What do you have? Use it faithfully, even the smallest thing and it will increase. This is a principle of God. Be responsible of what God has given you.

II Timothy 1:7, "For God has not given us a spirit of fear, but of power and love and a sound mind" K. J. This is a key verse in being a good steward. Be faithful in using your mind. You have the right to decide what thoughts you think. You are responsible in what decisions you make. Be faithful and take that responsibility. The little things in your life are so important. Nothing, absolutely nothing is too small, too unimportant to not be taken seriously. They all make a difference. One little choice, one decision, one word, can make all the difference.

Being a steward starts with your time. Decide how much time you have to work on something, then stop. The same with your money, how much do you want to spend for a certain thing - then stop, until later. Do this in everything in your life, things no one else knows about, your strength, your very thoughts. It is not something that makes the front page of the newspaper. But it is very important!

The Promise: to a faithful steward, always more is given

The Condition: Being able to make a decision and doing it. Being honest with yourself, knowing that there is a God in heaven. Not only is He seeing what you do, but He is ready to help you always.

Take time to memorize the verse. Write it on a card, carry it with you, repeat it many times a day. Also memorize the reference. Read Luke 16:1 -13, every day this week.
Let the word become flesh - a part of you!

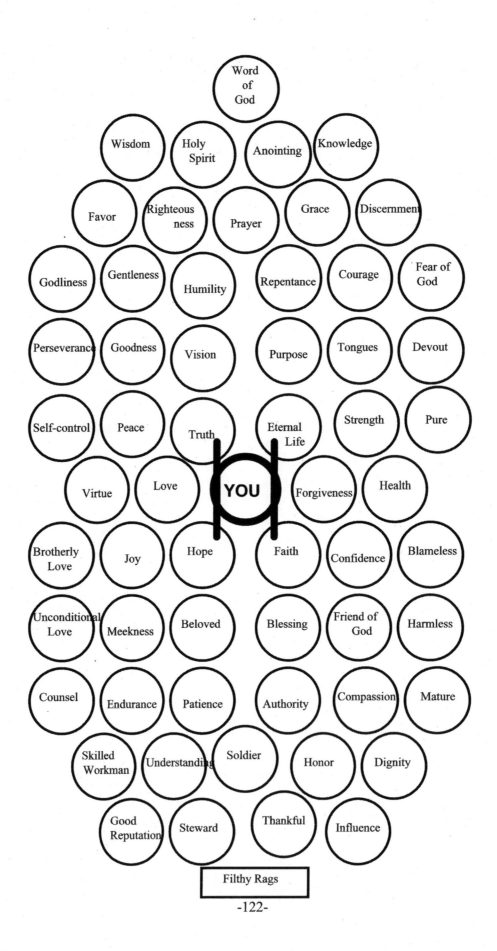

Good Reputation

**Jesus Christ is the same
yesterday and today,
yes and forever.
Hebrews 13:8**

To have a good reputation consists of being consistent, a person that is reliable. Thinking of a good reputation, who has a better reputation then Jesus Himself? He lived what He was sent to do. This we can find in Luke 4:18, "The Spirit of the Lord is upon Me, because He has anointed Me to preach the gospel to the poor, He has sent Me to proclaim release to the captives, and recovery of sight to the blind. To set free those who are downtrodden, to proclaim the favorable year of the Lord." At the end of His time on earth, John 19, "When Jesus therefore received the sour wine, He said, 'It is finished!' He bowed His head, and gave up His spirit," His work as a man was done. This is a good reputation.

He is still the same. Philippians 1:6, He is still doing the things He was sent to do. He is doing it through His body, the church, (you and me). Hebrews chapter eleven talks of many who lived and died and left a good reputation behind. Hebrews 11,12 and 13 are the whole summary of what Hebrews is telling us. It is the practical part of Hebrews. This is how what has been said works in our lives. Every verse in chapter thirteen is rich enough to preach a sermon from. You would greatly benefit from studying these 3 chapters.

Hebrews is showing us all about Jesus. Let me give you a short outline.
Chapter 1 - (v.1-3) the divinity of Christ; (rest of chapter) Christ superior to angels
Chapter 2 - Christ superior to humanity   ---   Chapter 3 - (v. 1-6) Christ superior to Moses
Chapter 4: (4:14- 5:10) He is a better High Priest   ---   Chapter 8,9,10 - The plan of Salvation
Also Hebrews there are 5 warnings, which are as follows:
1. (2:1-4) danger of neglect (neglect so great a salvation)
2. (3:7-4:13) danger of hardening of the heart   ---   3. (5:11-6:20) danger of dullness of hearing
4. (10:26-39) danger of shrinking back   ---   5. (12:25-29) danger of refusing God
Reading through from chapter 1-10 leaving out these warnings will gave you a very good picture of our Lord. Then go back and read the warnings. After you have done all this, you will get more out of the summary, 11,12, and 13.

The Promise: a good reputation

The Condition: to be conformed to the image of Jesus (Ro.8:29)

Take time to memorize the verse. Write it on a card, carry it with you, repeat it many times a day. Also memorize the reference. Read the entire chapter of Hebrews 13, every day this week.
Let the word become flesh - a part of you!

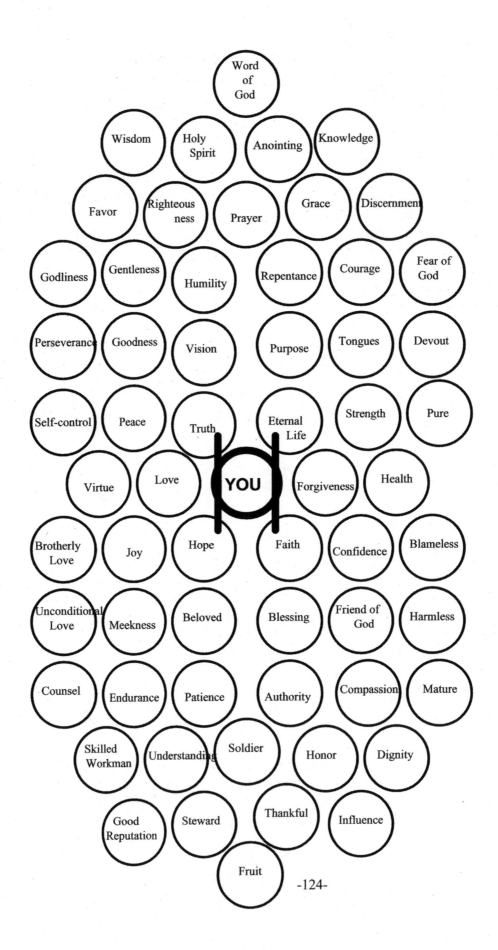

Word of God

Wisdom Holy Spirit Anointing Knowledge

Favor Righteousness Prayer Grace Discernment

Godliness Gentleness Humility Repentance Courage Fear of God

Perseverance Goodness Vision Purpose Tongues Devout

Self-control Peace Truth Eternal Life Strength Pure

Virtue Love YOU Forgiveness Health

Brotherly Love Joy Hope Faith Confidence Blameless

Unconditional Love Meekness Beloved Blessing Friend of God Harmless

Counsel Endurance Patience Authority Compassion Mature

Skilled Workman Understanding Soldier Honor Dignity

Good Reputation Steward Thankful Influence

Fruit

-124-

Fruit
(In Every Good Work)

**so that you may walk
in a manner worthy of the Lord,
to please Him in all respects,
bearing fruit in every good work
and increasing in the knowledge of God.
Colossians 1:10**

Fruit is produced when the right thing is done at the right time. Timing is important, staying in tune with God. John 15:4, we cannot bear fruit of ourselves, unless we abide in Jesus. Reading the Word, praying, staying sensitive to the Holy Spirit is the way we will know what God's plan is for each day.

Colossians 1:9-14, is a prayer. Use it for yourself, and for those you love. It is when you are "filled with the knowledge of His will," that you are able to do what the Father is doing. To produce fruit in your life, you must do what God is doing. And remember: He is more concerned about what you are becoming then what you are doing.

Ephesians 2:8-10, makes it very clear. We are saved by grace, not by works, but then we are, "His workmanship created in Christ Jesus for good works," (v.10). God has a work He wants you to do. Here again we need to remember that it is the little things that matter. That there really are no big things, but everything is a series of small things. And that preparation makes the difference in a crisis.

You now have 60 mighty blessings (men) walking with you, in whatever comes your way in life. This is not the end of God's blessings, it is only a start. My prayer for everyone who has worked through this book to this point would be: that you would understand that you are not walking this journey on earth alone. And in any difficulty that might come up in your life, you would be able to be so prepared that you would bear fruit, rather then fall apart. Think about that!

Always remember that you are "looking for a city which has foundations, whose architect and builder is God," even as Abraham and Sarah. (Hebrews 11:10) As you walk on this journey, you will be more and more conformed into the image of Jesus.

The Promise: bearing fruit in every good work

The Condition: walking in a manner worthy of the Lord, to please Him in all respect, increasing in the knowledge of God, being strengthened with all power, giving thanks to the Father.
Take time to memorize the verse. Write it on a card, carry it with you, repeat it many times a day.
Also memorize the reference. Read the entire chapter of Colossians 1, every day this week.
Let the word become flesh - a part of you!